A TREASURY OF SCIENCE JOKES

by

Morris Goran

Illustrated

THE LINCOLN-HERNDON PRESS INC.
818 South Dirksen Parkway
Springfield, Illinois 62703

A TREASURY OF SCIENCE JOKES

First Edition

Manufactured in the United States Of America.

For information write to:

The Lincoln-Herndon Press, Inc.
818 South Dirksen Parkway.
Springfield, Illinois 62703

Library of Congress Cataloguing in Publication Data.
Library of Congress Catalog Card Number: 86-081524
ISBN 0-942936-09-4 (Softcover):

TABLE OF CONTENTS

Introduction

This book contains all kinds of humor-stories, one-liners, puns, funny riddles and even knock-knocks. It covers many sciences and could just as well have been called "A Treasury Of Science Jokes For Non-Scientists" because all the material is understandable. There are no technical jokes for the specialist. Ethnic and off-color ones are also avoided. In all cases, however, the joke is given in bare essentials. The user, whether layman, scientiest, teacher or student can embellish to suit his needs.

WARNING

This book may be hazardous to your sense of humor unless read in small amounts at one time.

1
AGRICULTURE

A farmer is a man with a sense of humus.

The milking machine has displaced the man who used to take things into his own hands.

Knock, knock.
Who's there?
Annapolis.
Annapolis who?
Annapolis a fruit.

The turnip is a plant that can't be beet.

A tangerine is a loose-leaf orange.

Hiram: What did you give your mule for distemper?
Zeke: Turpentine.
[One week later]
Hiram: I gave my mule turpentine and it killed him.
Zeke: Yep. Killed mine, too.

Why don't grapes ever get lonely? They hang around in bunches.

What is the first thing a farmer plants in his garden? His foot.

What fruit is on our 25-cent coin? The date.

Knock, knock.
Who's there?
Cantaloupe.
Cantaloupe who?
We cantaloupe tonight; my father is watching.

Beets are potatoes with high blood pressure.

Cauliflower is college-educated cabbage.

Artichokes are loose-leaf asparagus.

Prunes are plums that have seen better days.

Teacher: What is the best way to raise potatoes and onions in a dry year?
Student: I would put the two crops in alternate rows. The onions would make the potatoes' eyes water, so both crops would be irrigated.

The radish is one vegetable that speaks for itself.

Blackberries are red when green and purple when black.

Pineapples are neither apples nor the fruit of the pine.

The peanut is neither pea nor nut; it's the fruit of a vegetable.

Teacher: Give me a sentence using the word "bean" three times.

Student: My father grows beans, my mother cooks beans and we are all human beans.

Cross a tobacco plant with a Mexican jumping bean and what do you get?
A Cigarette that flicks its own ashes.

Cross bluegrass with sword grass. When the wind blows your lawn will cut itself.

If you cross a crocodile with a cucumber will you get a crock of pickles or a pickled croc?

Eggs are the only food that comes naturally in no-deposit, no-return, bio-degradable packaging.

The cow gives all the milk it can. Farmers can all the milk it gives.

How do you get a sound between a squish and a splash? Squash a squash.

Step on a bunch of grapes and you get a whine.

A California forester experimented with Eucalyptus trees, trying to find new uses and open new markets. He talked a railroad vice president into buying a thousand railroad ties made from the trees.
Apparently they weren't satisfactory. A month later he received a one-word letter from the vice president: "Dear Sir: Eucalyptus."

Fruit is always on the limb.

Banana skins are golden slippers.

Celery is what you get for working.

When lemons give a dance they have a sourball.

A prize cow won so many blue ribbons it wound up in a mooseum.

Ag professor: Can you tell me how long cows should be milked?
Smart student: The same way you milk short ones?

Mother cabbage to little one: You must learn to overcome storms, drought, rabbits, bugs and pollution. Then you will grow.
Little one: When should I quit growing?
Mother: Quit when you're a head.

Corn and potatoes are like sinners of old. They have ears and hear not; they have eyes and see not.

Sign in a supermarket:

LETTUCE WILL NOT TURN BROWN IF YOU PUT YOUR HEAD IN A PLASTIC BAG BEFORE PLACING IT IN THE FRIDGE.

Headline on news story about riots in Belgium:

BRUSSELS SPROUTS REVOLT

Onions build you up physically, but they sure can tear you down socially.

The number of pedestrians who got hit by cars this year increased 100%.
It was a bumper crop.

Farmers measure corn by the bushel and the peck. City folks measure it by the fifth. On television it's measured by the hour.

One man's corn is another man's bourbon.

Raisins are just grapes with a lot of worries.

Rhubarb is celery with high blood pressure.

Little boy: Dad, could I use Cheerios as seeds and raise doughnuts?

When insects attack the crop, potato farmers keep their eyes peeled.

The cranberry farmer was easy-going; he knew his arguments would bog down.

"The tartness of his face sours ripe grapes." Shakespeare, *Coriolanus*

Little corn to Mom corn: How did I get here?
Mom corn to little corn: The stalk brought you.
Little corn to Mom corn: You mean there's no Pop corn?

Asparagus is a vegetable that is served with one end braided.

"Now that pH meter is designed for use in the field. Note the sensing tip is protected to prevent hay fever."

When does a farmer need a plumber? When there are leeks in his garden.

———————

What is yellow and writes? A ballpoint banana.

———————

Why is the watermelon so full of water? Because it's planted in the spring.

———————

When does the farmer hurt the corn? When he yanks its ears off.

———————

If wheat could talk it would scream, "Help! He's reaping me!"

———————

The dairy farmer told the truth when he said, "All I am I owe to udders."

———————

Mushrooms grow in damp places. Is that whey they're

shaped like umbrellas?

From a city reporter's account of a rural accident:
When Farmer Brown's truck overturned on the bridge, the entire load of wheat was dumped into the river.
Brown's accident may have been caused by a blinding headache. Witnesses at the scene said he was clutching his head while shouting, "Migraine, migraine!"

From a pupil's essay: Farmers in Oklahoma raise Alpaca grass. They irritate it to make it grow.

Apples look alike when pared.

A farmer became a city policeman. He was given a beet.

Two fruit growers merged their orchards and made a perfect pear.

There's a new mail-order company that sends the vegetable-of-the-month to its customers by parsley post.

Will Rogers said, "We have the onion to make us cry; it's too bad we don't have a vegetable to make us laugh."

Let's hope it isn't true that the man with the hoe never gets as far as the man with the hokum.

Chickens are the only animals you eat before they are born and after they are dead.

What turns without moving? Milk.

The hardest kind of bean to raise on a farm is a jelly-bean.

Auto driver at farmer's market: "Can you make a U-turn?"
Farmer: "No, but I can make her eyes pop."

2
ANIMAL BEHAVIOR

A cheerful old bear at the zoo
Could always find something to do.
    When it bored him, you know,
    To walk to and fro,
He reversed and walked fro and to.

What did the monkey say when his sister had a baby?
"Well, I'll be a monkey's uncle!"

What did the cow say to the silo?
"Is my fodder in there?"

What makes the dog man's best friend? It wags its tail
instead of its tongue.

A fan magazine reports that a cat in Hollywood is so
rich from doing television commercials that it supports
three human families. It recently bought its own tuna
fishing fleet.

A talking dog became a television comedian. One night
he was performing on a late-night talk show when a
large dog came on and dragged him off the stage.
Just before he went off-camera he managed to say,
"Sorry, folks. It's my mother. She always wanted me to
be a doctor."

Cross a flea with a rabbit and what do you get? Bugs Bunny.

_____

Cross a fish with an elephant and what do you get? Swimming trunks.

_____

Little girl: Do cats go to heaven?
Mother: No, cats don't have souls.
Little girl: Then where do angels get their harp strings?

_____

A village governing board once proposed an ordinance that would require dogs, cats, canaries and chickens to be silent from ten p.m. to six a.m. Discussion ended when one member said, "I'm all for this ordinance, if someone will tell me how we get the noisy critters to read it."

_____

Where do cows go on dates? To the moovies.

_____

How is a horse like a bartender? It gives its bit and listens to every woe.

_____

Why are rabbits never bald? They're always raising hares.

_____

Why is a rabbit's nose so shiny? Its powder puff is on the wrong end.

_____

Six cows are walking in line. Which one can say, "There are five cows behind me?" None. Cows can't talk!

_____

A skunk once challenged a lion to a fight. The lion declined, saying, "You would gain fame fighting a lion while everyone who met me for a month afterward would know I had been in the company of a skunk."

A kangaroo went to see a psychiatrist because he wasn't feeling jumpy.

A jet-setter is a fast-flying bird dog.

A romantic cat is a smitten kitten.

A horse placed a bet on himself to win. The bored cashier took his money and gave him a ticket without comment. After the race the horse came back to collect his winning. He said, "Aren't you surprised I can talk?" The cashier said, "No, but I sure as heck didn't think you could win."

Teacher: Where is the elephant found?
Johnny: I didn't think anything that big could get lost.

How do you stop a charging elephant? Take away his credit card.

Said the ram to the sheep, "I love ewe."

Said the bull to the dairy farmer on a cold morning, "Give these ladies a nice warm hand!"

One laboratory rat said to another, "I've finally got him conditioned. Every time I press this bar and stand on my head he gives me a piece of cheese."

Two show-biz celebrities were talking. "Whatever happened to your talking dog?" asked one. The other said, "I had to get rid of him. It was bad enough when he wanted top billing, but then he made out his own income tax return — and listed me as a dependent."

The only time you succeed by passing the buck is when you're racing a deer.

Skunks never get rich. They just make a few scents.

Two lions started fighting during a card game after one called the other one a cheetah.

A man was cornered by a lion. He began to pray. To his surprise the lion began to pray, too. The man said, "What have you got to pray about?" "Quiet," said the lion, "I always say grace before a meal."

Mr. and Mrs. Rabbit were being chased by wolves. "They're gaining on us. What shall we do?" said Mrs. Rabbit. "We'll stop here a few minutes," said Mr. Rabbit. "By the time they catch up we'll have them outnumbered."

Cross a chicken with a racing form to get a hen that lays odds.

Cross a mink with a robin and watch the fur fly.

Cross a cat with a Xerox machine and what do you get? A copycat.

A man and a dog walked up to a newsstand. The dog asked for a paper. The propieter said, "What! A dog that not only talks but reads!" "Aw, he ain't so smart," said the man. "He only looks at the comics."

A lady went into a department store to buy a sweater for her poodle. "What size, Madam?" asked the clerk. "Oh, dear," said the lady. "I don't know. He's about this tall." The clerk said, "Why don't you bring the dog in for a fitting?" "Oh, no," the lady said. "It's for his birthday and I want to surprise him."

Have you heard? The Three Little Pigs once did time in the pen.

The near-sighted turtle fell in love with a hard hat.

A tabby cat swallowed a ball of yarn and had mittens.

When a rabbit says "lettuce" it could be a vegetable or a proposition.

A pet pig was named Bad R 1. Its owner always explained that was his pen name.

A man on a fishing trip came into a camp a little the worse for beer. He encountered a bear and tried to give it a hug. The bear hugged the man and threw him against a tree. The fisherman picked himself up and said, "Just like a woman. Put her in a fur coat and she thinks she's too good for anybody."

A sourpuss is a cat that has swallowed a grapefruit.

Papa Bear and Mama Bear were watching tourists go by in their cars. Mama Bear said, "It's cruel to keep them caged up like that."

Two weevils started life together. One succeeded and

the other failed. The failure was the lesser of two weevils.

Once upon a time there were four young bulls. Three of them escaped from the farm. One went to Rome and became a papal bull. The second secured employment on Wall Street and became a stock market bull. The third went into retailing and became a bull in a china shop. The fourth just stayed on the farm for heifer and heifer.

A squid fell in love with an octopus. He was just a crazy, mixed-up squid.

When scientists established communication with dolphins the first thing they heard from a dolphin was "Don't you guys have anything better to do than sit around shooting the bull with us?"

A dentist tried to give an injection of novocaine to a rabbit.
"Oh, no! Not that, not the needle!" cried the rabbit.
"Why not?"
"I'm the ether bunny!"

How far can a dog run into the forest?
Halfway. After that he's running out.

What did the baby porcupine say when he backed into a cactus?
"Is that you, Mother?"

When the little boy asked, "Why does your dog walk in circles before going to bed?" his mischievous grandfather said, "He's a watchdog. He's winding himself up."

Horse sense is what keeps horses from betting on people.

———————

Never, never play leapfrog with a unicorn.

———————

Put lemon on your venison and you have sour doe.

———————

A dog applied for a job which called for excellent typing, computer skills and bilingual ability. The dog passed the typing test at 60 words a minute and operated the computer satisfactorily. The employer asked, "Are you really bilingual?" The dog answered, "Meow, meow."

———————

A duck, a frog and a skunk went to a movie. The duck got in with its bill, the frog with its greenback and the skunk with its scent.

———————

Cross a mink with an octopus to get a coat of arms.

———————

If you cross a rabbit with a porcupine you'll get sore hands.

———————

Cross a dog with a hen to get pooched eggs.

———————

Three bulls escaped from the pasture. The two large bulls were easily captured, but the small one was found miles away after a lengthy search. That's because a little bull goes a long way.

———————

Combine three-sevenths of a chicken, two-thirds of a cat and one-half of a goat. What do you have? Chicago.

———————

Why do elephants need trunks? They have no glove compartments.

What do you call elephants who ride in jet airplanes? Passengers.

A man and his dog were enjoying a movie. The dog barked for the hero, snarled at the villain and howled during the sad parts. A man in the next seat said, "I marvel at that dog's reactions to the movie." The man replied, "Me, too. He hated the book."

If you want a cat that can say its name, call it "Meow."

Cross a crocodile with an abalone and you've got a croc-abaloney.

Cross a hen with a banjo to get a self-plucking chicken.

What do you get when you cross a tiger with a parrot? Nobody knows, but when it talks everybody listens!

A man walked into a bar and sat between a dog and a cat. The dog said, "Well, so long, boys" and left. The man said to the bartender, "Did you hear that? That dog talks!" The bartender said, "Naw, dogs can't talk." The man insisted. "I heard him talk." The bartender explained, "It's just that crazy cat. He's a ventriloquist."

Why did the cat join the Red Cross? It wanted to be a first-aid kit.

Why did the goat eat fluorescent tubes? He wanted a light lunch.

What happens when two frogs go after the same fly? They get tongue-tied.

When should a pig be able to write? When it's turned into a pen.

Why do elephants trumpet? Because they have no talent for the violin.

A lion, a donkey and a fox returned from their hunt. The lion said, "Donkey, divide our kill into equal parts, one for each of us." The donkey carefully did as he was told. The lion killed the donkey, then turned to the fox and said, "Fox, divide our kill into equal parts, one for each of us." The fox made a huge pile of game for the lion, reserving only a crow for himself. The lion said, "How did you learn to divide so well?" The fox responded, "I just had a lesson from the donkey."

City boy (bragging): I'll bet you've never seen the Catskill Mountains.
Country boy: Nope. Just mice.

The earthworm said, "I love you. Will you marry me?" The answer was, "Shut up, you fool. I'm your other end."

Dog One: Bow Wow!
Dog Two: Meow!
Dog One: Are you crazy?
Dog Two: No, I've been studying foreign languages."

Skeptic: "How could Balaam's ass talk like a man?"
Believer: "It could be just as easy for an ass to talk like a man as it is for a man to talk like an ass."

The leopard said to the eye doctor: "Please examine me. I see spots every night." The doctor said "So what, you are suppose to see spots! You're a leopard." The leopard replied: "But I am married to a zebra!"

The musician approached the bear trainer after witnessing the circus bear play piano. "How did you ever get the bear to play piano?" he asked. "How do you get anyone to play piano?" said the trainer. "He took lessons."

Cow one: "I saw something I cannot get over."
Cow two: "What was it?"
Cow one: "The moon."

When does a horse act human? When it gives its bit readily and listens to every woe.

Cross a shark with a snowball and get frostbite.

Cross a sheep with a kangaroo and get a woolen jumper.

3
ANTHROPOLOGY

An anthropologist is a literate person studying illiterate people.

An archeologist is a scientist whose career lies in ruins.

Noah was the first archeologist.

Two men were arguing the merits of their ancestry. One said, "When your ancestors were sitting in trees cracking nuts with their bare paws, we came along and sold them nutcrackers." The other replied, "When your ancestors were eating wild berries in the forest, mine already had diabetes."

A mummy is a person pressed for time.

Cannibal: Shall I boil the new missionary?
Chief: No, he's a friar.

Is language called the mother tongue because women invented it or because they use it more?

An archeologist could send his spouse to an early grave with his little digs.

An anthropologist encountered a cannibal who had heard there was a war going on, with many dead and wounded every day. The cannibal inquired how the so-called civilized world could eat such enormous amounts of human flesh. The anthropologist explained that fallen enemies are not eaten. Said the cannibal, "What kind of barbarians are you—to kill without purpose?"

Two men were arguing about how far back they could trace their ancestry. One insisted he had records going back to biblical times. The other said he could go back to the Great Flood, when all records were lost.

Is an African with a ring in her nose any more a savage than an American with a pearl in her ear?

A member of a head-shrinking tribe returned from a visit to the city. Of all the wonders he described, tribesmen were most impressed with television, which he described as "a wonderful machine that shrinks entire bodies."

In some early societies natives beat the ground with clubs and yelled loudly. Anthropologists call this primitive ritual. We call it golf.

An Indian chief in Arizona installed electricity in the tribal restroom in 1927. He was the first man to wire a head for a reservation.

Our ancestors were overworked and undereducated. Are we underworked and overeducated?

Plato once described man as the only featherless biped. Diogenes pulled the feathers off a bird, held it up and proclaimed, "Behold! Plato's man."

Archeology is the science of digging around, trying to find another civilization to blame ours on.

_____

If Adam and Eve came back to earth, they wouldn't recognize anything—except the jokes.

_____

"Bone voyage", shouted the wife of the anthropologist as he left for an expedition.

4
ASTRONAUTICS

"But I can't have you along, shooting off your mouth, dear!—
The purpose of this flight is to fly faster than sound!"

"This is comparatively new to us, men . . . so I asked my neighbor's kids to give us a few pointers on our first test flight."

An astronaut is a whirled traveler. A cloud hopper.

Earth satellites are the latest exception to the idea that there is nothing new under the sun.

"It's a wire from the Atomic Energy Commission . . . they want you to keep your eyes peeled for any uninhabited planet . . . suitable for H-Bomb test . . . "

An astronaut is chosen for space travel because he has his feet on the ground.

Astronauts look clean-cut because their flights are scrubbed so often.

How do you put a baby astronaut to sleep? Rocket.
Picture an astronaut at the end of a lifeline knocking at the door of the space capsule: "What the ———do you mean 'Who's there'?"

What do astronauts do when they're dirty? Take a meteor shower.

Teacher: How can we ever send an expedition to the sun, where there is such intense light, heat and radiation?
Student: Send them at night.

The space age is here. We're all looking for space to park in.

When an astronaut gets angry, does he blast off?

Planet: The thing to do before taking off on a trip into space.

An astronaut is the only man hailed as a hero when he is down and out.

We're trying to find inhabitants on other planets because we can't get along with one another on earth.

Astronaut (to famous author):
I read your book while I was in orbit. I couldn't put it down!

"Our scientific preparations are complete, men . . . all we have to do is wait for a full moon so we'll have more room to land . . ."

The astronaut's favorite meal? Launch.

Astronauts find a place in the sun by reaching for the moon.

How did Mary's little lamb go to the moon? By rocket sheep.

Why is a prisoner like an astronaut? Both are interested in outer space.

Athletes get athlete's foot; astronauts get missile toe.

Why did Mickey Mouse go to outer space? To find Pluto.

Why are astronauts like pugilists? They're always seeing stars.

Those people who believe that the landings on the moon were hoaxes done in Hollywood follow in the footsteps of the ones who think the moon is an illusion staged by songwriters.

5
ASTRONOMY

An astronomer is a guy who stands around looking at heavenly bodies.

———————

The moon affects the tide—and the untied. ✓

———————

Why is a telescope like the Bible? Both are to be looked through, not at.

———————

Dough is like the sun; it rises when it's light.

———————

Two little boys looked into a well and saw a reflection of the moon. They concluded the moon had fallen in the well, and resolved to get it out. Using a rope with a hook on it, they began to pull. The hook caught on something and they pulled it loose with such force they fell to the goound facing the sky. "Look how far we threw the moon!" they said.

———————

There is no precipitation on the moon—except when it's waning.

———————

Her teeth are like stars; they come out at night. *false teeth*

———————

The moon went into a cloud bank; it was down to its last quarter.

"According to my figures, the next total eclipse will occur March 15th . . . when the income tax blots out most bank balances."

A man tried to buy a ticket for a trip to the moon. The travel agent told him all flights were cancelled because the moon was full.

The boy prodigy confessed he was so bright his father call him Sun.

___

The astronomy professor explained the students' lack of interest in his class by saying the subject was over their heads.

___

Teacher: Why does the sun get so big just before it goes down?
Student: It has sucked up all that daylight.

___

Teacher: What is the International Date Line?
Student: A marriage agency?

___

Her eyes are like stars—always blinking.

___

She has a very sunny disposition. Just standing close to her you can get a tan.

___

Planets are like .357 magnums; they're big revolvers.

___

Moonlighting is the sun's other job.

___

Teacher: What is the zodiac?
Student: It's the zoo in the sky where lions, goats and other animals go when they're dead.

___

Teacher: Which is farther, the moon or China?
Student: China. I can see the moon, but I can't see China.

___

Teacher: Define 'Earth's axis of rotation'.
Student: An imaginary line at the center of the earth's daily routine.

A telescope magnifies greatly, but not as much as a good press agent can.

What happened to the man who sat up all night wondering where the sun went when it set? It finally dawned on him.

First tourist: I got up at dawn to see the sun rise.
Second tourist: You couldn't have chosen a better time.

After explaining that the seasons are caused by the earth's inclination and its revolution around the sun the teacher asked Johnny to name the four seasons. The answer was, "Vinegar, mustard, pepper and salt."

Night falls daily but never breaks.

Millions of people would get up to see the sun rise if they had to pay for it.

The Milky Way is a celestial dairy.

Teacher: Do any of the planets affect our weather here on earth?
Student: Mercury does. It's in our thermometers.

Teacher: Describe the earth's daily movement.
Student: It makes a resolution every 24 hours.

Student: Is there intelligent life on Mars?
Teacher: Intelligent life on Mars is practically impossible—just as it is on Earth.

What keeps the moon from falling? Its beams.

What is the most important letter of the alphabet? The letter "e" is. It's at the beginning of eternity and at the end of time and space.

Which is lighter, the sun or the earth? The sun is. It rises every morning.

What's the best place to see an all-star show? A planetarium.

Boy: I'll get up when the first ray of sun strikes my bed.
Mother: Oh, no you won't. Your bedroom faces west.

Principal: I've been told you're advocating world revolution.
Teacher: All I said was, there's a revolution of the earth every year.

Student (on a test): Nathan Halley said, "I only regret that I have but one life to give to my country." This statement became known as Halley's comet.

Student (on a test): The Mare Imbrium and Mare Nubium are the horses that followed the cow that jumped over the moon.

Student (on a test): The equator is a menagerie lion running around the middle of the earth.

Mars is also known as the red barren.

The teacher explained the rotation of the earth. She concluded by saying, "At sunset the sun doesn't really go down. That's just a figure of speech." That evening the pupil was observing the sunset intently when his mother asked, "What are you doing out there?" His reply was, "I'm watching a figure of speech."

Teacher: Why does an eclipse occur?
Student: To give the sun time for reflection.

Teacher: What's the difference between the earth and the moon?
Student: The moon is like the earth, but even deader.

Teacher: Canis Major and Canis Minor are the dog constellations. There is also a dog star. What is its name?
Student: Lassie.

An amateur astronomer was looking through his telescope. His little boy came into the room just as a shooting star flashed across the sky. "Wow! What a shot!" the boy said.

A child saw the moon's reflection in a lake. "What is it?" he asked. "The moon," said his mother. The child thought a moment, then said, "How did we get up here?"

Sunrise! It's horizon shine time!

Corona: An officer who inquires into the manner of death.

True or false?
    Light comes from the sun.
    Feathers are light.
    Therefore feathers come from the sun.

Three brothers named Ray moved west to homestead. They asked their father to suggest a name for their place. He said, "Since the Rays converge here I think you should call it 'Focus'."

An astronomer is a night watchman.

Teacher: Which is more important, the sun or the moon?
Student: The moon. The nights would be too dark without its light. The sun shines by day, when we don't need it.

Teacher: My hat will represent Mars.
Student: Is Mars inhabited?

The sun is the oldest settler in the West.

Eclipse. That's what a gardener does to a hedge.

An astronomer's business is always looking up.

The earth is a minor planet with major problems.

Which came first, the sun or the shadow?

The comment of a student: "You couldn't get me to go to the moon if it was the last place on earth".

Cynics in one state of the United States claim that its four seasons are flood, mudslide, earthquake and hurricane.

Skylight—sun, moon and stars.

"The budget won't stand for a raise, Professor, but the board is willing to grant this concession in running your department."

A losing politician has a strong resemblance to the earth — flattened at the poles.

———————

The egotistical astronomer hitched his bragging to a star.

———————

Since Halley's comet was first portrayed in an Ice Age cave drawing it has been called the Ice Man Comet.

6
BACTERIOLOGY

A bacteriologist is a man whose conversation always starts with the germ of an idea.

_____

Fungus is a guy named Gus, always very funny.

_____

One germ said to another, "Don't bacilli."

_____

Before I heard the doctors tell
The dangers of a kiss,
I had considered kissing you—
The nearest thing to bliss.
But now I know biology
And sit and sigh and moan,
Six million mad bacteria—
And I thought we were alone.

_____

They say exercise kills germs, but how do you get them to exercise?

_____

Germ warfare is infecticide.

_____

Why does the sheriff call his small-town jail "amoeba"? Because it has only one cell.

_____

Two little amoebae swimming in the veins of a horse decided they were hungry. In their search for food they swam into the arteries. Trying to make headway against

the current, they died of exhaustion.
Moral: Don't change streams in the middle of a horse.

"I'll say it's tough running the camera microscope. Ever try getting a bacterium to say 'cheese'"?

Richard Nixon's downfall was caused by a staff infection.

Bacteria: The rear entrance to a cafeteria.

Bacteria are the only culture some children are exposed to.

An amoeba is a one-celled organism that multiplies by dividing.

Bacteria infecting a person's lymph nodes felt a sudden wave of anti-biotics. One of them said, "I'm going to hide in the liver." A second said, "I'm heading for the bloodstream." A third said, "I think we all should take the shortest way out of here."

7
BIRDS

Knock, knock.
Who's there?
Wendy.
Wendy who?
Wendy red, red robin comes bob, bob, bobbin' along.

How do the birds know you just polished your car?

The dove brings peace and the stork brings tax exemptions.

The goose is a bird that grows down as it grows up.

A football landed in the chickenyard. The rooster went over to it, studied it a while, then said, "Ladies, I'm not complaining, but look at the work they're turning out next door."

Sea gulls flying in tight formation are chorus gulls.

Today the dove of peace is a mockingbird.

The penguin is the only bird that dresses formally for every occasion.

A turkey doesn't eat Thanksgiving dinner; it's already stuffed.

After weeks of trying, the young entertainer got an appointment with a talent agent. "I do great bird imitations," he said. The talent agent yawned and said, "Sorry, there's no market for bird imitations." The youth pleaded, "Give me a chance. At least let me show you what I can do." The agent said, "No, it would just be a waste of my time."
So the youth got up and flew out the window.

Which bird can carry the most weight? The crane.

The bird with the largest bill is not the pelican, but the stork.

A pigeon-toed is a strange creature—half pigeon, half toad.

The hen is immortal; her son will never set.

The birds were flying south. One of the flock said to another, "Why do we follow that leader all the time?" The other said, "He's got the map."

One robin does not make a spring but one lark can cause a fall.

The crow is a real gentleman; he never shows the white feather and never complains without caws.

Teacher: When our national bird was chosen the field finally narrowed to the owl and the bald eagle. Why do you think the eagle won out?
Student: Because the owl didn't give a hoot?

Cross a turkey with a centipede and you'll have a

drumstick for everyone at Thanksgiving.

Cross a chicken with a bell and you get an alarm cluck.

Cross a mud hen with a clay pigeon to get offspring that lay bricks.

A man on a train had a basket of pigeons on the seat beside him. The conductor came through the car and said, "We don't allow any pets or livestock on this train." With that he opened the basket and allowed the pigeons to fly out the window.
The man said, "Those are valuable homing pigeons. I'm going to have a word with your supervisor when we get to Columbus."
"This train doesn't go to Columbus. We're going to Cincinnati," said the conductor.
The man stuck his head out the window and yelled, "Hey, fellows—Cincinnati, Cincinnati!"

A little girl watching a chicken plucker said, "Do you take their clothes off every night?"

A fowl ball is where chickens go to dance.

A rooster has a comb but no hair.

Why did the parakeet land on the fish's back?
He was looking for a perch.

Why do birds fly south?
It's too far to walk.

Why is a hen on a fence like a penny?
She has a head on one side and a tail on the other.

A customer in a pet shop tried for half an hour to get a four-thousand-dollar parrot to talk. The parrot didn't make a sound. The customer said to the shop owner, "If this parrot is so expensive why won't it talk?" The shop owner answered, "He doesn't want to be quoted."

The leader of a flock of geese turned and said to his followers, "Stop that infernal honking! It you want to pass, pass!"

Cross a rooster with an owl and get a cock that stays awake all night.

Cross a hen with an owl and get a bird that lays an egg every day and catches mice at night.

Cross a carrier pigeon with a woodpecker to get a bird that not only carries messages but knocks at the door when it arrives.

Mother: Did you behave yourself in school today?
Boy: Yes, I did.
Mother: Be careful. Lies get you into trouble.
Boy: How do you know I misbehaved?
Mother: Oh, a little bird told me.
Boy: Be careful about lies. Everyone knows birds can't talk.

On which side does the eagle have the most feathers? The outside.

What do ducks do when they fly upside down? They quack up.

What did the hen say when she laid a square egg?
Ouch!

A general encountered a colonel who was wearing extra eagles on his uniform. The general gave the colonel an angry dressing-down for being in a non-regulation uniform. "What possible reason could you have for wearing extra eagles?" he demanded. The colonel said, "It's the mating season."

The stork is a distributor allied with an infant industry.

A scarecrow is a figure that tries to achieve an effect without caws.

The crow perched on a telephone wire to make a long-distance caw.

Headline on a story reporting a rise in the price of goose feathers:

DOWN IS UP

Cross a carrier pigeon with a parrot. If the offspring ever get lost they can ask for directions.

Cross a chicken with a waitress to get a hen that lays tables.

Little boy: Why does those big turkeys walk like that?
Grandfather: That's called strutting. They strut because they're proud.
Little boy: I bet they wouldn't strut so much if they could see what's ahead for them at Thanksgiving.

How do hens and roosters dance? Chick to chick.

Why does a crane standing in the water raise one leg?
If it raised the other leg it would dunk itself.

A chicken farmer annoyed his neighbor, a turkey farmer, with his constant shop talk. The turkey farmer tried to change the subject, but the chicken farmer talked on and on about chicken houses, chicken roosts and chicken feed. The turkey farmer, exasperated, went home to dinner.
His wife said, "Did you have a nice talk with our neighbor?" He said, "No. That man simply won't talk turkey. He's too chicken-hearted for me."

A turkey farm has a gobblestone driveway.

The woodpecker is a knocking bird.

Why are birds so nervous in the morning?
Because their little bills are all over dew.

The rooster crows but the hen delivers.

Fowl language is what you hear coming out of a chicken house.

A hen is the only one who can lay down on the job and still get results.

Q: Cross a duck with a cow and what do you get?
A: Milk and quackers.

Q: Cross a dog with a chicken and what do you get?
A: A pooched egg.

What is the difference between unlawful and illegal?
An ill eagle is a sick bird.

An eavesdropper is a kind of bird.

A duck walks as though it had been riding on a horse all day.

The baby bird poked his head out of the shell, looked around, and went back.

8
BOTANY

Botany is the science in which plants are known by their aliases.

The newsletter of a gardening club carried this announcement of the impending visit of a famous botanist:

> Dr. Greenthumb will lecture on wildflowers of the region and conduct the ladies on a walk through the park, identifying each by shape and fragrance.

If roses are red and violets are blue, then what color is a belch? Burple.

What flowers might you find in a zoo? Dandelions and tiger lilies.

What room cannot be entered? The mushroom.

Give a dandelion an inch and it takes over a yard.

Teacher: Describe pruning.
Student: Pruning is cutting off dead twigs so the trees will bear prunes.

College joke books are the howls of ivy.

Frank: I took my girl to see a tree farm.
Ernie: Was it fir?
Frank: Only about five miles.
Frank: I mean—cedar trees?
Ernie: Of course we cedar trees.

Frank: No, tell me. Juniper?
Ernie: Once or twice. But she wasn't in the mood.

———————

Teacher: Some plant names have the word "dog" as a prefix. Two of them are dogrose and dogwood. Can you give other examples?
Student: Collie flower!

———————

Grass grows by inches and dies by feet.

———————

Nurseries are so called because baby plants, like baby humans, must be nursed. So far no one has found out how to burp a petunia.

———————

When two trees are talking and another listening, the third tree is leavesdropping.

———————

The only means of self-protection for a flower is its pistil.

———————

It was the last question on the last exam before Christmas vacation: "How did life originate?" The student wrote, "God knows. I don't. Merry Christmas." When he got his paper back after the holidays he found this inscription, "God gets 100. You flunk. Happy New Year."

———————

If quinine is the bark of a tree is canine the bark of a dog?

———————

How many sides are there to a tree? Two. Inside and outside.

———————

Why is the willow weeping? It feels sorry for the pine tree pining.

A woman heard that her neighbor was the grand prize winner in the local garden club. She asked, "How do you account for your success? Do you have a green thumb?" Her neighbor said, "No, just trowel and error."

Gardeners are professional grafters.

Florist: The plant in the green pot belongs to the gardenia family.
Customer: Are you taking care of it while they're on vacation?

A gold digger is a tomato that needs a lot of lettuce.

Cooks have thyme on their hands.

Life is ova before it begins.

A man went to a floral shop to buy anemones. The florist didn't have any. Being a clever salesman, he persuaded the man to buy ferns instead. When the man got home he told his wife, "I bought ferns, even though I wanted anemones." His wife said, "With fronds like these, who needs anemones?"

A nursery owner put in a garden tool repair shop so he could make mower money.

Sign in a florist's shop:

ALL OUR PLANTS CONTAIN
CHLOROPHYL

Is the Brazil nut a wild man who lives in the Amazon jungles?

Flowers are the laziest of plants. They are usually found in beds.

Trees have been called feminine because they do a striptease in the fall, go with bare limbs all winter, get a new outfit every spring and live off the sap all summer.

What can you say when your flowers don't bloom? "Up-sadaisy."

Sap is a sign of vitality in all trees — except the family tree.

Said the flower to the bee, "Don't bug me."

Teacher: Isn't it remarkable how fast trees grow?
Student: Not to me. They don't have anything else to do.

Books come from trees. That's why we have branch libraries.

What animal can jump higher than a tree? Any animal. Trees can't jump.

Advertisement for a plant nursery:

WE ARE YOUR
GROWING CONCERN

Acorn: A sore caused by a tight shoe.

Bigotry: A larger tree.

"To protest environmental pollution, I will take in carbon dioxide but not give off oxygen."

A man was arrested for talking dirty to plants. He was caught making an obscene fern call.

———

Garlic is like a plucky prizefighter.
It does its best fighting after it's down.

———

Roses speak the language of love but tulips do a much better job.

———

Rosebud: What brought me here?
Rose: The stalk.

———

What is the craziest tree? Knotty pine.

———

Tree to lumberjack: Please, leaf me alone.

Autumn is when Mother Nature turns over a new leaf.

_____

When is a tree frightened? When it's petrified.

_____

People who buy a lot of books on gardening become good weeders.

_____

If all the cars in the United States were pink, the United States would be a pink carnation.

_____

Life started from a cell and if justice is done some of it is going to end there.

_____

The best garden club is a hoe handle.

9
CHEMISTRY

*"Please, sir, we've got to find the money for a centrifuge. My wife claims we're **ruining** her Mixmaster . . . "*

A green little chemist
On a green little day
Mixed some green little chemicals
In a green little way.

The green little grasses
Now tenderly wave

57

Over the green little chemist's
Green little grave.

Oxygen is pure gin. Hydrogen is gin and water.

How do you protect against high temperatures? Asbestos you can.

Teacher: What is H_2O?
Student: H, I, J, K, L, M, N, O.
Teacher: What kind of an answer is that
Student: You said "H to O."

What would you give to a person who has just taken hydrogen cyanide? The last rites.

A chemist refused to work with acetates because he believed he who acetates is lost.

Reprinted with permission of Markson Science.

"With each order, you get a newly-discovered element. Offer is limited."

Kings always sat on their gold. Who sits on silver? The Lone Ranger.

_____

A famous wine expert bragged he had never tasted water. He even brushed his teeth with vermouth. When asked why he abhorred water he said he had an iron constitution and water would rust his pipes.

_____

A chemist who wanted to be rich went to work for a perfume company. He made a lot of scents.

_____

You can miss the silver lining by expecting gold.

_____

Iron was discovered because someone smelt it.

_____

"You definitely need a new graduated cylinder. Especially if your old one still has Roman numerals."

"It's the new story of the decade—Lab goes one whole day without anyone breaking any glass."

Customer: I want some consecrated lye.
Druggist: You mean concentrated.
Customer: It does nutmeg any difference. You know what I camphor. How much does it sulfur?
Druggist: I never cinnamon with so much wit.
Customer: I should myrrh-myrrh. You see, ammonia novice at this.

Ice is an example of hard water.

If H_2O is hot water, then CO_2 is cold water and CH_2O is sea water.

Argon is immediately north of California.

How do you make anti-freeze? Hide her woolen pajamas.

Student: Why isn't there any hydrogen in Ireland?
Teacher: Hydrogen is abundant everywhere. How did you get such an idea?
Student: It's right here in the textbook — "There's no hydrogen in the free state."

"Whaddya mean, get out of your Erlenmeyer flask? I'm Erlenmeyer."

Reprinted with permission of Markson Science.

RENFREW
LABS

"Your first project is to develop a chemical substance that will cure all known diseases. Then, after lunch . . ."

Reprinted with permission of Markson Science.

A man wrote to a government bureau to ask if he could use hydrochloric acid for cleaning boiler tubes. The answer was, "Uncertainties of reactive processes make use of hydrochloric acid undesirable where alkalinity is involved."

The man wrote to thank the bureau, saying he would use the acid. He received a letter that began, "Regrettable decision involves uncertainties. Hydrochloric acid will produce submuriate invalidating reactions." Again the man thanked the bureau for letting him know it was OK to use hydrochloric acid.

By return mail he received a letter saying, "Hydrochloric acid will eat hell out of your tubes."

A psychoceramist is a crackpot.

A chemist who falls into acid gets absorbed in his work.

Chlorine is a dancer in a night club.

Copper is a policeman.

Antimony is the money collected by ex-wives.

Two men in a bar were filling up on free snacks during happy hour. "Boy, these little hot dogs are good," said one, eating his 16th. Then he began to yawn and nod off. "I'm so sleepy," he said. His buddy replied, "It must have been that last barbiturate."

Carbon: The storage place for city buses.

Barium: What you do with dead people.

Tin: Not fat.

Oxide: Shoe material.

Teacher: Is there a universal solvent?
Student: No.
Teacher: Why not?
Student: There's no container.

Very good

Student (on a test): The combination of oxygen and other elements is called constipation.

A chemist driving to the lab happened to see a car run over a rabbit. He stopped, got out of his car and revived the rabbit with smelling salts. A bystander said, "What did you use to make that rabbit hop away?" The chemist grinned and said, "Hare restorer."

Miscible: Very unhappy.

Ba (Na) 2S: Bananas.

The metallic age is when you have silver in your hair, gold in your teeth and lead in your feet.

The human body has enough salt to season 25 chickens, enough chlorine to sanitize five swimming pools, enough lime to whitewash one fence, enough glycerine to make a jar of nitro, enough magnesium for ten flashlight bulbs, enough fat to make ten bars of soap, enough iron for one small nail and enough sulfur to conquer the fleas on one Yorkshire terrier.

Ad headline:

WE DO WELL WATER AND
AFFLUENT ANALYSIS

Fehling solution: What the professor uses when a student makes below 70 on the final exam.

Why do chemists use nitrates to make explosives? Because nitrates are cheaper than day rates.

A chemist saw this news headline: POLICE SEEK LEAD IN GOLD THEFT. He said to his wife, "The police force must have a staff alchemist."

Woman to judge: I want my freedom and I also want ammonia.
Judge: You mean alimony. Ammonia is used to wake people up.
Woman: Getting money out of him will wake him up.

Flattery is soft soap and it's 90% lye.

Glycerine: A vicious liquid, miserable in water in all proportions.

Headline in a farm paper: Ag suppliers seek silver lining.
(Did the writer know "Ag" is the chemical symbol for silver?)

A perfume salesman puts his business in other people's noses.

Prospector: I'm looking for uranium.
Bartender: What does uranium look like?
Prospector: I dunno. I've never seen any.
Bartender: How can you find uranium if you don't know what it looks like?
Prospector: Did you ever hear of Columbus?

Boron is what a teacher shouldn't be.

Today's flowers are polypropylene, polystyrene, plexiglass and vinyl.

Zinc — that's what happens if you don't know how to zwim.

Chromium covers a multitude of tins.

The toughest chemistry prof on campus was famous for his acid test.

Knock, knock.
Who's there?
Ammonia.
Ammonia who?
Ammonia bird in a gilded cage.

The dye makers' convention met in a tint.

Two chemists were looking at a pretty girl. "Just like any human, she's 90% water," said one. Said the other, "Yes, but what surface tension."

An ad ruined by a typographical error:

EFFECTIVE REPELLENT
FOR SHARKS, BEAVERS
AND WATER RATES

Scientists in the Naval Research Laboratory developed a new hair dye. They established a bleach head.

A semi-conductor is someone who leads the orchestra once in a while.

Zinc—that's where you put the dirty dishes.

Litmus is a lye detector.

Ad for the Copper Development Association:

COPPER ROOFING — NOTHING TOPS IT

Student (on test): It's easy to tell an Erlenmeyer flask from a Florence flask. Florence has a round bottom.

A chemical laboratory director was showing a musician around the place. He said, "There's nothing I can do about the bad odor. I apologize." The musician said, "A bad odor for a chemist is like dissonance for a musician — momentarily unpleasant, but essential to the work."

Astatine was named after the dog in the movie "The Thin Man."

Nobel invented dynamite and established a booming business.

Calcium: What Cal said when she saw Um.

The chemistry professor's dog was a laboratory retriever.

Coal goes to the buyer and then to the cellar.

When someone asked the unemployed chemist why he wasn't working he shrugged and said, "I have no retort."

On the examination paper of a student who had transferred to chemistry from theology school: "Paraffin is the next order of angels above seraphins." In his laboratory notebook he wrote: "To collect the fumes of sulfur hold a deacon over a flame in a test tube."

The stockbroker misunderstood and called a chemist to investigate what he heard were asset-based reactions.

A romantic song title for a chemist contains the names of the nobel gases: "When night krypton and the stars argon, the moon radon, then you xenon".

"I don't care who you are. You're trespassing in my flame test!"

Reprinted with permission of Markson Science.

10
COMPUTERS

The computer is a marvelous machine that is quick as a wink without having to think or go for a drink.

Do computers have good manners? They take small bytes.

They took the computer to a psychiatrist. It had a screw loose.

There's a police sergeant who still talks about the print-out he got the first time he put a suspect's name in the computer—"I'm not programmed as a stool pigeon."

"Do what it says . . . PUNT!"

Fish 'n' chips: An automated tuna fleet.

Do human beings like computers? They turn them on.

A young man got off to a bad start on his new job when he accidentally gave his boss a printout that read, "Elsie Smith in the Investment Department is the fairest one of all."

A perfect computer would be able to call its own repair-man.

Someone dropped a rubber band into the computer; now it makes snap decisions.

The computer didn't eliminate red tape; it only perforated it.

Computer chips are small because computers take small bytes.

Computers are for the terminally involved.

Smash computers and let the chips fall where they may.

A computer is a machine that is dumber than a human and smarter than a programmer.

Computers can solve many problems, but not the ones where things don't add up.

What does a baby computer call its father? Data.

Digital computer—Someone who counts on his fingers.

Headline:

SCIENTISTS DEVELOP COMPUTER PROGRAM
THAT STIMULATES OIL RESERVOIRS

Computer mating is a form of dater processing.

Cross a computer with a midget and get a short circuit.

Where does a computer keep its money? In its memory bank.

The only computer that can be produced by unskilled labor is the brain.

We'll know we've created artificial intelligence when we have a computer that blames its mistakes on another computer.

A lady mistook her food processor for her word processor and got minced words.

Necessity is the mother of invention. Bread is a necessity; the computer is an invention. Therefore, bread is the mother of the computer.

There's an important difference between data and information. Data is 382436. Information is 38-24-36.

A computer will surely die if it has a terminal illness.

"What bonehead asked it to solve Russian-American relations?"

11
GEOLOGY

A geologist is a fault finder.

Geology is a subject that brings students down to earth.

Geologists' favorite lullaby—"Rock-a-by Baby." Favorite treat — rock candy. Favorite dessert—marble cake.

Petrology is the study of the gneiss places on earth.

A diamond is class in glass.

A dinosaur is a colossal fossil.

A cave is a dearth of earth.

The Grand Canyon is the hole of fame.

First man: What did you do this summer?
Second man: Worked in Des Moines.
First man: Coal, iron or gold?

A cliff dweller is just another bluffer.

An iceberg is a permanent wave.

A creek is a river with low blood pressure.

A fjord is a Scandinavian automobile.

A geyser ruled Germany until 1918.

Diamonds don't grow on trees but they're frequently found on limbs.

Mountain climbers always want to take another peak.

To spot a glacier you must have good ice sight.

Conundrum is a mineral found in Canada.

A mountain range is a cookstove used at high altitudes.

A bore is a kind of river pig and a delta is the man who looks after it.

Quartz is made up of pints.

On or about March 21 comes the venereal equinox.

Ferdinand Magellan was the first man to circumcise the earth.

Any prospector knows panning for gold is not lodes of fun.

A diamond is a coal that stuck to its business.

A diamond is one of the hardest things on earth—to get back.

Do rivers sleep in river beds?

He: What a view from this restaurant at the edge of the canyon!

She: A wonderful gorge.
He: Yes, I could have done without dessert.

The man who discovers a lead and zinc mine can rest on his ores.

If you're just a pebble on the beach to the opposite sex, be a little boulder.

If you climb to the top of an active volcano you can see the crater smoking.

Where does a geologist go to relax? To a rock concert. What if he can't hear the music? He's stone deaf.

An earthquake is a topographical error.

A glacier is a man who puts glass in windows.

Gneiss is a rock that's not bad.

The Sahara Desert is a vast nomad's land.

What's the laziest mountain in the world? Mt. Everest.

What's the scenery like at a canyon? Gorge-ous.

A cartographer can always be caught mapping.

An intelligent crevice would be a wisecrack.

An earthquake struck a California town during city council meeting. The members left without a proper adjournment. Later the city clerk added this sentence to the official minutes, "The council adjourned on the motion of City Hall."

"Looks like old Cactus Joe struck some uranium ore."

A river, like some people, has a mouth bigger than its head.

The volcano song is "Lava, come back to me."

What did one mountain say to the other? "Let's meet in the valley."

Why is a hill like a lazy puppy? It's an inclined plane—a slope up.

A seaside hotel advertised proudly that it was "practically on the level."

A geyser occurs when Mother Nature is steamed up about something.

A volcano is a mountain that blows its stack.

Mud thrown is ground lost.

What runs but never walks? A river.

What does a volcano do with its lava? Throws it up.

When is coffee like soil? When it's ground.

It's not easy to tell a real cliff from a bluff.

A geyser is a well with hiccups.

Some trees are petrified. Ground water, rain and wind have rocked them.

What has a mouth and a fork but never eats? A river.

Why are rivers rich? Every river has two banks.

What do you call the little rivers that run into the Nile? Juveniles.

A hill is a piece of ground with its back up.

A river delta is a mouth full of mud.

A geyser is a waterfall that goes up.

The mineralogist is the only living creature that belongs to the mineral kingdom.

An eye doctor traveled to Niagara to see the largest cataract in the country.

Mining is a vein pursuit.

A flood occurs when a river gets too big for its bridges.

The world really is getting smaller. More and more people are walking on it, wearing it down.

Baby thought: Just because they sprinkle me with powder they expect me to talc.

Hawaii has a lot of volcanoes. Ash holes everywhere!

One rock to another: Schist a minute.

_____

"Let's shake," said the lake meeting the earthquake.

_____

The geologist's wife was cold as marble because he took her for granite.

_____

Does a geologist have rocks on his mind—or just rocks in his head?

_____

Gneiss bands don't make punk rock.

12
HUMAN ANATOMY

Samuel Butler's description of the human body:

A pair of pincers set over a bellows and a stew pan and the whole fixed on stilts.

Abdomen—Men from the invisible planet Abdo.

Arthritis—Twinges in the hinges.

Customer: See if the chef has pig's feet.
Waiter: I can't tell; he has shoes on.

What do you call it when you stub your toe? A toe truck.

Sign in window of maternity shop:

CLOTHS TO MAKE
YOUR HEIR LESS APPARENT

A tongue is like a race horse; it runs fastest when it carries least weight.

Dandruff—Small, whitish scales trying to get ahead.

The heart is an organ kept in a trunk and played by beats. It's most enjoyable when lost or given away.

Your lap is another thing you can't take with you.

———————

Flat feet—The arch enemy.

———————

Compliment a bald man; tell him he has a beautiful head of skin.

———————

The abdomen contains the organs of indigestion.

———————

Your larynx is always down in the mouth.

———————

The widow of 19th-century physiologist Rudolph Virchow compared husbands to teeth. "It's hard to get them and while we have them they give us a great deal of pain and trouble. But once we lose them they leave a wide gap."

A paunch is surplus gone to waist.

The mouth is the glutton's friend, the orator's pride, the fool's trap and the dentist's salvation.

You don't get a peptic ulcer from what you eat, but from what's eating you.

Perspiration is a liquid impossible to drown in.

God gave us two ears and one tongue so we'd listen twice as much as we talk.

The lip can slip, the eye can lie, but the nose knows.

It's an unusual medical book that has no appendix.

Knock, knock.
Who's there?
Eileen.
Eileen who?
Eileen down to tie my shoelaces.

Teacher: Which are the last teeth to appear in the mouth?
Student: False.

When is a nose not a nose? When it's a little reddish.

What did one eye say to the other? There's something here that smells.

What did one toe say to the other? Don't look, there's a heel following us.

In some countries it is the custom to kiss the newborn on the part of the body associated with future fame. You kiss the baby on the forehead if you want it to become a philosopher, on the mouth if you want it to become an orator, on the throat if you want it to become a singer. What part of the body must have been kissed to produce an excellent chairperson?

Of all the parts of the body the tonsils have the best social life. They are taken out so often.

You may fall in love with a dimple but you marry the whole girl.

When the teacher's glass eye fell in the basin and went down the drain he said, "There goes another pupil."

Fifth-grade student (on a test): The Abominable Cavity contains the bowels, of which there are five—A, E, I, O, U.

Is my nose running? No, it's still on your face.

What part of the body can you hold in your left hand but not your right?
Your right elbow.

The gingerbread man with a vision problem wore contact raisins.

Deliver—a vital organ of the body

_____

If a man still has his tonsils, adenoids, appendix and hernia he's probably a surgeon.

_____

Why does Santa's belly jiggle when he laughs? 'Tis the season to be jelly.

_____

What animals go wherever you go? Your calves.

_____

Third grader (on a test): The borax is between the brain and the abominable cavity.

_____

What is as big as you and weighs nothing? Your shadow.

_____

Why can't a nose be 12 inches long? It would be a foot.

_____

When brains were passed out he thought they said "pains."

_____

What part of your anatomy is long and hard, and sticks so far out of your pajamas you can hang your hat on it? Your head.

_____

Doctor: Do you have any scars on you?
Patient: No. Sorry, just a few cigarettes.

_____

Patient: I'd like to have that nasty little wart removed.
Doctor: The divorce lawyer is on the third floor.

_____

Why can't a locomotive sit down? It has a tender behind.

Fourth grader (on a test): Aesophagus is the author of Aesoph's fables.

Her jokes are like her eyes—only cornea.

What do dentists call their formal dances? Gumballs.

"Someone came to see you this morning."
"Did he have a bill?"
"No, just a regular nose."

"During the war a bullet went clear through my chest, front to back."
"Not through your heart?"
"No, my heart was in my mouth."

Television has too many commercial breaks; they've become a compound fracture.

Small-town newspaper headline:

MRS. SMITH'S FALL ON ICE
HURTS HER SOMEWHAT

From a letter—Since I saw you last I've had my appendix taken out and a new refrigerator put in.

Anatomical oddities—The girl who cried her heart out. The man who lost his head. The man who couldn't put his foot down. The girl who was all ears. The fellow who didn't have a leg to stand on. The man who keeps his nose to the grindstone. The man who has one foot in the grave. The chap who keeps a stiff upper lip. The woman who stewed in her own juice.

13
HUMAN BEHAVIOR

Man is the only animal that goes to sleep when he isn't sleepy and wakes up when he is.

Do you hunt bear? Not in cold weather.

In spring boys feel gallant and girls feel bouyant.

Customer: I'd like some talcum powder.
Clerk: Walk this way, please.
Customer: Miss, if I could walk that way I wouldn't need talcum powder.

A little boy was sobbing because his dog was gone. "I'm so sorry you lost your dog," said his aunt. "I didn't lose him," said the boy. "He lost me."

Cleanliness is next to godliness, but in childhood it's next to impossible.

A psychoanalyst treats himself by lying on a couch and talking to himself.

An adult has stopped growing vertically and started growing horizontally.

Habits are fragile; you can't drop one without breaking it.

". . . And as a visionary of long standing I can promise you bigger and better mirages than my opponent . . ."

Turn green with envy and you're ripe for trouble.

Love is a binge; marriage is the hangover and divorce the remedy.

Paradox—Two physicians.

Wife: Why do you call me "Angel?"
Husband: You're always flitting about, forever harping on things and constantly insisting you don't have a thing to wear.

A couple sent out a cryptic announcement—"Isaiah 9:6." Most of their friends and relatives sent gifts by return mail, but some took a few days to figure it out. Isaiah 9:6 begins, "For unto us a child is born, unto us a son is given." Their baby, named Isaiah, weighed nine pounds, six ounces.

Husbands and wives are like fires; neglect them and they go out at night.

A neurotic is a person in a clash by himself.

A child psychologist is a kid who knows how to handle his parents.

Manic-depressive—Easy glum, easy glow.

Nurse: What did the doctor tell you to do for your arthritis?
Patient: He said I should get bed rest and take aspirin.
Nurse: Fine. That will be forty dollars.
Patient: I won't pay it.
Nurse: Why not?
Patient: I'm not taking his advice.

Whistler found his mother on the floor and said, "Are you off your rocker?"

A cool person is one who can look like an owl after acting like a jackass.

A jury is a group selected to decide who has the better lawyer.

A race track is the only place where windows clean people.

Psychiatrist: Mr. Smith, you've got to stop believing you're a fly.
Smith: I know, but how can I convince myself?
Psychiatrist: The first thing to do is climb down from the ceiling.

A clergyman whose wife had just died wrote to the bishop. "I regret to inform you that my wife died yesterday. I would be grateful if you would send a substitute for the weekend."

A preacher who had just moved to town put this sign in front of his church:

UNDER NEW MANAGEMENT

Man (to his mistress): I have a terrible marriage. My wife understands me.

Television in summertime is deja view.

He gave her a piece of his mind — and had nothing left.

All the hardships of this world
Might wear you pretty thin,
But they won't hurt you, one least bit
Unless you let them in.

A man brought his young son to the office of a congressional committee and said, "I think you can use him. He does nothing all day long but ask questions."

A news story began, "During the grave diggers' strike local cemeteries will be manned by skeleton crews."

The teacher thought she had heard everything until a mother asked that her children be forgiven for their backtalk because they were diabetic and took insolence every morning.

In today's world you have to be crazy — or else you'll go nuts.

Patient: I think my trouble is stress on the job.
Psychiatrist: What do you do?
Patient: I sort oranges by size—small, medium and large.
Psychiatrist: I don't see how that could cause stress.
Patient: You don't? All day long it's decisions, decisions, DECISIONS.!

With amnesia you don't know where you're going. That's the big difference between amnesia and magnesia.

When the little boy's mother brought a new baby brother home he asked, "Are you going to trade me in?"

A physician applying for a post as ship's doctor had to

pass an oral exam. The first question was, "What if the captain faints on the bridge?" "I'd bring him to," the doctor said. "What if he's still wobbly?" "I'd bring him two more."

___

Sign in a psychiatrist's office:

SATISFACTION GUARANTEED
OR YOUR MANIA BACK

___

First man: Get off my foot!
Second man: Oh, sorry.
First man: Look Fatty, why don't you put your foot where it belongs?
Second man: Don't tempt me!

___

A man swamped by paperwork went to an efficiency expert. Next day he came to the office and found 25 letters to answer. He followed the expert's advice. He answered the first letter while drinking three martinis and dumped the remaining 24 in the wastebasket without a qualm.

___

P. O. clerk: This package is too heavy. It needs more stamps.
Customer: You mean more stamps will make it lighter?

___

The teacher began her explanation of the theory of relativity by saying that an object looks large when close and small when far away. A wise guy in the first row said, "You mean from such stuff Einstein made a living?"

___

Teacher: To what class of animals do I belong?
Student: Ma says you're a cat and Pa says you're an old hen.

Why did the little moron tiptoe past the medicine cabinet?
He didn't want to wake the sleeping pills.

A woman wrote to a newspaper:

> I have a dog that growls, a parrot that swears, a stove that smokes and a cat that stays out all night. Do I need a husband?

Teacher: Use the word "extinct" in a sentence.
Student: If the human race disappeared from the earth, you could say the human race is extinct—but who would you say it to?

A real egotist is a guy that would like to die in his own arms.

A delegation of women went to see the president of the local college. They said, "Some of the women students don't pull down their shades as they prepare for bed. The scene tends to distract our husbands." The college president's reply was, "I suggest it would be simpler for you to pull down your own shades."

Sign in a barber shop window:

HAIRCUTTING WHILE YOU WAIT

Too many light-heads think headlights cause accidents.

Some people have no respect for age unless it's bottled.

If you want to know yourself, run for public office.

"My dog is smart."
"How do you know?"
"I asked him how much is two minus two and he said nothing."

The neurotic builds castles in the air, the psychotic lives in them and the psychiatrist collects the rent.

"I do desire we may be better strangers." Shakespeare, *As You Like It*

Doctor: I can't quite diagnose your trouble. I think it's too much drink.
Patient: OK, I'll come back when you're sober.

Mother (showing off her child for company):
    What does the cow say?
    Moo, Moo.
    What does the dog say?
    Bow wow.
    What does the duck say?
    Quack, quack.
    What does mommy say?
    No, No.

A man on a park bench was tearing his newspaper to bits and letting the confetti blow all over the ground.
A bystander said, "Why on earth are you doing that?"
"To keep the elephants away."
"Man, there are no elephants within a thousand miles of here."
"See? It works."

A young man went to a computer dating service and specified he wanted someone who enjoyed water sports, liked company, was comfortable in formal clothes and was short. The computer matched him with a penguin.

A confession is a bad time story.

A gossip has a good sense of rumor.

"Better a witty fool than a foolish wit." Shakespeare, *Twelfth Night*

"Were I like thee, I'd throw away myself." Shakespeare, *Timon of Athens*

Woman: My husband thinks he's a chicken.
Psychiatrist: How long has this been going on?
Woman: Two years.
Psychiatrist: Why did you wait so long to seek help?
Woman: We needed the eggs.

The greatest underdeveloped territory on earth is under your hat.

When someone speaks straight from the shoulder you often wish his words came from a bit higher up.

A Platonic lover is someone who gazes at the eggshell while someone else eats the omelette.

Barber: How shall I cut your hair?
Client: In silence.

A woman told her husband to see a psychiatrist when he threw away his shoes because they were sticking out their tongues at him.

Quarreling, bickering, greed, jeolousy!—Supposing Mars doesn't have any inhabitants—What can I lose?

A speaker annoyed by a heckler in the audience told this story:

When I was a child my father gave me a pet donkey. I promised I'd care for it diligently, but I left the gate open and the donkey wandered off. It tried to cross the railroad track and was killed by a train. My father and I looked sadly at the remains. He said, "Son, this donkey will haunt you forever." AND THERE'S THE JACK-ASS NOW!

She was such a prude she went into a closet to change her mind.

He was afraid of dying, so he stayed in the living room.

Ignorance is when you don't know and somebody finds it out.

Teacher: Your son is incorrigible. I know of a club that would help.
Parent: Never mind, I've got a baseball bat.

In our "advanced" civilization we don't beat drums to ward off evil spirits, but we blow horns to break up traffic jams.

There was a young lady in Ealing
Who had a peculiar feeling
That she was a fly
And wanted to try
To walk upside down on the ceiling.

There was a young fellow named West
Who dreamed he was being suppressed.

When he woke up he
Discovered a puppy
Had fallen asleep on his chest.

Don't complain about your lot in life; build on it.

The worst part about being idle is that you can't take time off.

From a coach's peptalk:

> Remember, football develops individuality, leadership and initiative. Now, get out there and DO EXACTLY WHAT I TELL YOU.

A psychiatrist finds you cracked and leaves you broke.

A man is like a worm; he wiggles a bit, then some chick gets him.

What's the difference between a psychotic and a neurotic?

A psychotic thinks two and two make five. A neurotic know that two and two make four—but he just can't stand it.

On his first day in kindergarten a boy began to cry. "What's the matter," said the teacher. "Are you home-sick?" "No," said the boy, "I'm heresick."

A dentist and a physician shared an office. Their receptionist was very pretty and both men were attracted to her. When the dentist went out of town on a five-day trip he put five apples in her desk drawer.

Judge: "Your wife claims you have not spoken to her in five years. Why?
Man: "I felt that I should not interrupt".

What is black and white and red all over?
Among the choices are a newpaper, a wounded nun, an embarrassed zebra, Santa Claus coming down a dirty chimney, and a skunk with diaper rash.

What goes in hard and dry and comes out soft and wet?
Chewing gum.

Clubs are appropriate for unruly children when kindness fails.

Businessman: Podunk University enrolls only football players and prostitutes.
Angry Client: My wife is a graduate of Podunk University.
Businessman: What position did she play?

Nurse (to doctor): There's a woman on the phone. You told her she was in false labor. Now she wants to know how to tie a false unbilical cord.

A blind man with a guide dog entered a department store. He picked up his dog by the tail and swung it over his head. An alarmed clerk hurried over and said, "May I help you?" The blind man said, "No, thanks, I'm just looking around."

A man falling off a cliff clutched a protruding branch and hung on desperately. He turned his eyes to heaven and cried, "Is anyone up there?" A voice from the clouds said, "Yes, my son. Let go of the branch and I will bear thee up." The man called out, "Anyone else?"

It's better to keep your mouth shut and appear stupid than to open your mouth and remove all doubt.

Why did the Creator make the first man before making the first woman? Because He didn't want any advice on how to do it.

Sigmund Freud was the famous Austrian physician who pioneered the study of the unseen by the obscene.

A boy hit his thumb with a hammer. He gritted his teeth in pain but didn't cry. His mother hurried to him and said, "Why aren't you crying?" He said, "I didn't think you were home."

A man in a tavern boasted he could outwit any robber. A highwayman who overheard followed the man from the tavern and accosted him. "I challenge you to outwit me," he said. "It's just you against me." The man answered, "Don't lie to me. I see your partner behind you." The robber turned to look and the man over-powered him with a surprise attack.

Is kleptomania catching? No, it's stealing.

A neurotic is a self-taut person.

A fishmonger told a customer, "Fish is good brain food. Buy these three herring at fifty cents each. Eat them and improve your intelligence." The customer bought the herring and came back the next day. He com-plained, "I'm not any smarter than I was." The fishmonger said, "You didn't eat enough. Here are six herring at one dollar each." The man bought the six her-ring. He was back the next day, saying, "Those herring still didn't make me any smarter."

"Still not enough," said the fishmonger. "Here are ten herring. You can have them for two dollars each." "Heck no," the man said. "That's too much money." "See?" said the fishmonger. "Now you're getting smart."

Witness: I was wedded to the truth.
Attorney: I infer that you're a widower."

Intuition is insight information.

A witness testified, "I heard the collision but didn't see it." The judge said to the jury, "Disregard this man's testimony. It's not good evidence." While the judge's head was turned the witness whistled loudly. "I'll hold you in contempt," the judge said. "Did you see me whistle?" said the man. "No, but I heard you," said the judge. The man said, "Not good evidence."

Two hooligans met an old woman driving two asses to town. They greeted her, "Good morning, mother of asses." She replied, "Good morning, my children."

If the first atom splitters had been children the reaction would have been, "Now you put that right back together again!"

A rabbit's foot is a poor substitute for horse sense.

A psychologist was refused service in a bar. He was too Jung.

Even the most beautiful model can't get work if she's a mannequin depressive.

Psychiatrist: Your wife has lost her mind.
Man: No wonder. She gave me a piece of it every day for twenty years.

A man had a friend who was a professional comedian. "Come with me to the Comedy Club Banquet," said the comedian. The man accepted. He enjoyed the food and conversation. Then, after dessert, each member rose in turn and reeled off numbers while the others laughed.

"What's happening?" said the man. "They're telling jokes by the numbers," the comedian said. "The Club has a joke file. To save time we don't tell the jokes — just give their file numbers. When your turn comes say 7563. That's a surefire laugh."

When the man's turn came he rose confidently and said, "7563." There was dead silence. The man sat down and said, "Not even a chuckle. What's wrong?" The comedian said, "Some people know how to tell a joke and some don't."

Judge (to witness): You lie so clumsily I advise you to get a lawyer.

A woman called the Fidelity Insurance Company and asked how much it would cost to insure her husband's fidelity.

When they were newlyweds his little dog ran around barking while his wife brought him his slippers. Now his little dog brings the slippers and his wife barks at him.

A cab driver painted one side of his cab blue and other red. Now if he has an accident the witnesses will give contradictory descriptions.

Doctor: Do you ever get up with a jerk?
Patient: I'm not even married.

"I'm going to sneeze at you."
"At who?"
"Atchoo."

Teacher: If I lay an egg on the table and lay two eggs on the chair, how many eggs will that be"
Student: I don't think you can do it.

First drunk: We'll never make it down these stairs.
Second drunk: I'll turn on the flalshlight and you slide down the beam.
First drunk: I'm no fool. When I'm halfway down you'll turn the light off.

A psychiatrist thought he'd heard everything; then a patient said, "I always sprinkle my pillow with sugar so I'll have sweet dreams."

Roses are red,
Violets are blue.
I'm schizophrenic
And so am I.

Letter from a great-grandmother:

> My hair is white and I'm almost blind,
> The days of my youth are far behind.
> My neck is stiff, can't turn my head,
> And I listen hard to hear what's said.
> My legs are wobbly, can't hardly walk,
> But, glory be, I sure can talk.
> And this is the message I want you to get:
> I can still get around, I ain't dead yet.

A yacht is called "she" because there's a lot of bustle about her and a gang of men around. It's not the initial expense that breaks you, it's the upkeep. When she's all decked out it takes a good man to handle her right. She looks smart topsides and she hides her bottom. When coming into port she always heads for the buoys.

A chemist's description of human beings:

Occurrence: Almost everywhere on earth, seldom in a free state.
Physical properties: Many colors, shapes, sizes and ages.
Chemical properties: Very active. Possess an affinity for gold, silver, platinum and precious stones. Activity greatly stimulated by addition of alcohol. CAUTION— Explosive in inexperienced hands.

An anthropologists's account of child behavior:

After the baby begins to crawl and walk it picks up so much dirt relatives dare not kiss it. It's Nature's answer to the false belief there's no such thing as perpetual motion. It can swim like a fish, run like a deer, climb like a squirrel, balk like a mule, bellow like a bull, eat like a pig and act like a jackass.

The child is skin stretched over an appetite. It's a noise covered with smudges. Like a tornado, it comes when unexpected, hits where least expected and leaves everything a wreck.

The child is a growing animal of superlative promise — to be fed, watered and kept warm — a joy forever, an occasional nuisance, the problem of our times, the hope of a nation. Every child born is evidence that God is not yet discouraged.

"That's our new laboratory rack. As I was saying, I'm a firm lab director . . . "

Reprinted with permission of Markson Science.

A zoologist's description of the human race:

Man is treacherous as a snake, sly as a fox, busy as a bee, slippery as an eel, industrious as as ant, blind as a bat, faithful as a dog, gentle as a lamb, drunk as an owl, still as a mouse, nervous as a cat, stubborn as a mule, thirsty as a camel, strong as an ox, vain as a peacock, happy as a lark, slow as a tortoise and crazy as a loon.

Humans can be led like sheep. They are chicken-livered, lion-hearted and pigeon-toed. They have the memory of an elephant, the beak of a buzzard, the arms of an ape, the eyes of a hawk, the neck of a bull and the shoulders of a buffalo. They have a whale of an appetite, a cat-like walk and a mousy manner.

Male and female alike can roar like a lion, coo like a dove, hop like a sparrow, work like a horse, fly like a bird, run like a deer, swim like a duck and drink like a fish. They play possum, stick thir head in the sand like an ostrich and act like a dog in the manger. They get hungry as a bear, wolf their food, parrot each other, play like a puppy, strut like a rooster and chatter like a magpie.

On the bulletin board of a nursing home:

> I can live with my arthritis
> And my dentures fit fine.
> I can see through my bifocals,
> But I sure miss my mind!

14

HUMAN PHYSIOLOGY

Alcohol will make you well when you're sick and sick when you're well.

———————

Patent medicines are seldom what they're quacked up to be.

———————

Aspirin is what you take when you can't take it any longer.

———————

A tranquilizer is a pill for the body to treat an ill of the mind.

———————

An alcoholic buys tranquilizers by the fifth.

———————

Amphetamine is the pick-me-up that lets you down.

———————

Sign in a drugstore: "We dispense with accuracy."

———————

Graffiti in restroom of an international airport:

URINATION OF STRANGE PEOPLE.

———————

"Have you ever been treated by a doctor?" "No, they always make me pay."

"Who cares if spinach makes me have big muscles . . . Does it increase resistance to atomic radiation?"

Blind man: How goes it?
Lame man: As you see.

***

"You're a hundred years old today. To what do you owe your long life?"
"I can't say. I'm still negotiating with two breakfast food companies."

***

The picture of health requires a happy frame of mind.

***

An alcoholic wants to feel fit as a fiddle and gets tight as a drum.

***

A baby is an alimentary canal with a loud voice at one end and no responsibility at the other.

***

An alcoholic sponge never fills up on water.

***

Knock, knock.
Who's there?
Urologist.
Urologist who?
Urologist a buncha nuts.

***

The label on the bottle said GUARANTEED TO MAKE HAIR GROW. A customer came in to get his money back, but the barber refused. The man had twelve inches of luxuriant bristles on his hairbrush.

***

Why did the simpleton fall on his knees to cough?
His doctor prescribed a cough drop.

***

"Do you know your forefathers?" "I had only one father."

His mother said "Cut it out" so often he became a surgeon.

A hangover is the wrath of grapes.

A cold can be either positive or negative. Sometimes the "ayes" have it, sometimes the "noes."

Teacher: What are hiccups?
Student: When somebody is percolating.

When the surgeon told the minister he should have his gall bladder taken out the minister replied, "What God hath joined together, let no man put asunder."

Indigestion is the failure to adjust a square meal to a round stomach.

The only thing that can be guaranteed to stop falling hair is the floor.

You count good health as the greatest blessing, but only when you're sick.

Infection often starts from scratch.

The obstetrician is another bird that delivers babies and has a large bill.

Signs in a sperm bank:

DEPOSITS WITHDRAWALS
JOINT ACCOUNTS FROZEN ASSETS

A wife looked at her husband's paunch and said, "You ought to diet."
"Yeah?" he said. "What color?"

She: I feel wonderful. I took a bath in milk.
He: Pasteurized?
She: No, just up to my chin.

The co-ed pleaded with the professor for a higher grade, saying, "I'll do anything for an 'A'". But the professor refused to put the heart before the course.

Man can live without air for seconds, without water for days, without food for weeks — and without ideas for years.

"All right, Murdock. What's this about a breakthrough in the field of cloning?"

Knock, knock.
Who's there?
Cirrhosis.
Cirrhosis who?
Cirrhosis are red and violets are blue.

Labor contractions are birthquakes.

The father was watching a baseball game on television when his son asked, "Is measles catching?" The father said, "No, Jones is."

Sign over a health spa:

THINNER SANCTUM

Protein is a movement in favor of teenagers.

She had so many varicose veins she went to the masquerade as a road map.

An apple a day keeps the doctor away; a clove of garlic a day keeps everyone away.

Hormone: The blending of several pitches in a musical chord.

What does a cow have four of that a woman has two of? Feet.

What does a dog do that a man steps into? Pants.

What great man was born on January 1? No man. Only babies are born.

A mother told her five-year-old son, "If you keep sucking your thumb you'll blow up and burst." Next day in the supermarket the boy saw a pregnant woman and said, "I know what you've been doing!"

First drunk: I feel dizzy but you're the one who's staggering. Why?
Second drunk: Alcohol affects the weakest member— in my case the feet, in your case the head.

Hardening of the arteries could be a highway resurfacing program.

An allergist treats patients for one wheezin' or another.

Masseuses are people who knead people.

Crying little boy: Mother, I fell down and sprained a liniment.

Gray hair is a reason for sighs.
So are crow's feet around your eyes.
But when your mind makes a contract your body can't fulfill,
You're really over the hill.

Said the real estate agent selling land to an eye doctor for his new clinic, "Now this is a site for sore eyes."

BandAid is a fund for needy musicians.

Successful dieting is just mind over platter.

A lot of people can't count calories. They have the figures to prove it.

A doctor who loses patience loses patients.

When Abraham Lincoln was president he contracted smallpox. He said, "Now that I have something to give everybody, nobody comes near me."

At family reunions there are lots of antibodies.

Better to hunt in fields, for health unbought,
Than fee a doctor for a nauseous draught.
The wise, for cure, on exercise depend;
God never made his work for man to mend.
—John Dryden

Abortion is a kind of Russian soup.

Mickey Mouse has Disney spells.

A man was so obsessed with Beethoven and his music that he opened the composer's coffin. The corpse opened its eyes, held up a large gum eraser and said, "Close the lid. I'm decomposing."

Three men were arguing about how far back a person can remember. The first man said he remembered being fed at his mother's breast. The second said he remembered his mother saying, as she went into labor, "I hope it will be a boy." The third said he remembered going to a picnic with his father and coming home with his mother.

Why is it? You can catch cold but you can't catch warm.

Doctor: Drink water thirty minutes before going to bed.
Patient: I can't. I'm full within five minutes.

Teacher: What does it mean to die intestate?
Student: It's when you die of bellyache.

A man locked himself outside the house, so he ran around and around it until he was all in.

Husband: What are you doing to my wife?
Lifeguard: I'm giving her artificial respiration.
Husband: Give her the real thing. I can afford it.

The difference between ammonia and pneumonia is that one is in bottles and the other in chests.

She was on a seafood diet. When she'd see food she'd eat.

Prisoner: You'll never keep me in jail.
Sheriff: What makes you think so?
Prisoner: I eat lox.

How do you avoid falling hair? Jump out of the way.

A new mother complained, "The worst part is holding the ice bag to my breasts to keep the milk fresh."

A doctor told a rheumatic patient to avoid all moisture and dampness. Six months later the patient said, "Can't you modify the treatment? I'd like to take a bath."

"How many pancakes can you eat on an empty stomach?"

"About eight."
"No, only one. Your stomach isn't empty after that."

"Let's go see that new movie, 'The Optimist'."
"Naw, I don't want to see a documentary about an eye specialist.

Student (on a test):
A sure way to detect tuberculosis is by X-ray or a horoscope.
The thorax first expands and then expires.
The digestive juices are bile and sarcasm.

Resurrection is when people are almost drowned and you revive them by punching lightly on their sides.

To revive a person who has fainted, lay them on their back until conscience returns.

Milk will never turn sour if you keep it in the cow.

Three kinds of blood vessels are arteries, veins and caterpillars.

Inspire — When you breathe in. Expire — When you don't breathe.

The permanent set of teeth has eight canines, eight cuspids, two molars and eight cuspidors.

The spinal column is a long bundle of round bones. Your head is on top and you sit on the bottom.

The three kinds of blood vessels are the veins, arteries and artilleries.

Teacher: What is the main difference between the digestive system of a cow and the digestive system of a human?
Student: Give water to a cow and she makes milk; it's the other way around with a person.

How does one avoid auto-infection? Drive with the windows open.

Kidnapping is when parents have a chance to get some sleep.

College-bred — A four-year loaf made with the yeast of youth and the old man's dough.

Doctor: Stop drinking brandy. It's your worst enemy.
Patient: The Scriptures command us to love our enemies.

Doctor: How is the little boy who swallowed the quarter?
Nurse: No change yet.

A hard drinker hid a bottle of whiskey under his nightshirts because it was a nightcap.

Don't drink milk at bedtime. You may wake up with a hangover. When you toss from side to side the milk turns to cheese, the cheese to butter, the butter to fat, the fat to sugar, the sugar to alcohol—and your're drunk.

The doctor ordered a local anesthetic. The nurse returned several minutes later to say, "We don't have a local anesthetic. The only one I can find was made in Sweden."

The digestive system is like a government; if it's a good one you don't even notice you have it.

15
INSECTS

Why do bees hum? They don't know the words.

A butterfly is a worm that turned.

A beehive is a sting ensemble.

A myth is a small moth.

One flea to another: Shall we walk or take a dog?

Take a lesson from the enterprising mosquito. He never waits for an opening; he makes one.

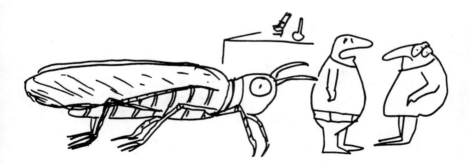

"Initial test show that you'll have to re-think the formula for that insecticide . . . "

"Wife: What's that crawling on the wall?
Husband: A ladybug.
Wife: What eyesight!

———

Why not shoo the mosquitoes? It costs too much. Let them go barefoot.

———

The termite woke up screaming when he heard somebody sing "I Dreamt I Dwelt in Marble Halls."

———

The pregnant bedbug will have her baby in the spring.

———

I've never seen a talking dog but I've seen many a spelling bee.

———

The largest ants are gi-ants.

———

Clerk: We don't have a single bedbug in this hotel.
Guest: No, they're all married with large families.

———

The archives are where Noah kept his bees.

———

There are three sexes — male sex, female sex and insects.

———

There was a young fellow from France
Whose hobby was searching for ants,
'Til he took quite a spill
On a tiny red hill,
And wound up with ants in his pants.

———

One termite to another: This will bring down the house.

———

Newly hatched termites are babes in the wood.

A pretty young maid from the kitchen
Found lying in grass so enrichin'
But she didn't figger
On meeting a chigger;
Now the maid from the kitchen is itchin'.

A scientist trained a flea to jump at the sound of a buzzer. He removed the flea's legs and sounded the buzzer. The flea didn't jump. He wrote, "When a flea's legs are removed the flea becomes deaf."

If we adopt the metric system what do we call the inchworm?

Knock, knock.
Who's there?
Amos.
Amos who?
Amos quito bit me.

Bugbear—an insect that crawls on bears.

How did the ant get its reputation as a hard worker? It always has time to go to picnics.

A mosquito doesn't get a slap on the back until it goes to work.

The potato bug is a beetle that plays on the tuber.

A bedbug is an undercover agent.

The wasp is one insect that knows how to make a point.

A caterpillar is a worm in a fur coat.

———————

An exterminator is a hired killer who doesn't go to jail.

———————

The humbug is an insect that wants to sing but doesn't know the words.

———————

The moth is one insect that enjoys chewing the rag.

———————

A mothball is a dance around a patio light.

———————

Two silkworms had a race and ended up in a tie.

———————

A neurotic insect is a jitterbug.

———————

Why did the moth eat a hole in the rug? He wanted to see the floor show.

———————

With no money to invest, he started a flea market from scratch.

———————

Termites never die. They live happily ever rafter.

———————

Two centipedes were walking hand in hand . . . in hand . . . in hand . . .

———————

A cocky roach is an arrogant bug.

———————

Why did the fly fly? The spider spied 'er.

———————

If flies are flies because they fly and fleas are fleas because they flee, then bees are bees because they be.

Colonel: I believe in fighting an enemy by using the enemy's own weapons.

Private: How long does it take you to sting a wasp?

The bee is such a busy soul
He has no time for birth control.
That is why in times like these,
We have so many sons of bees.

Why did the exterminator hold his ears?
He couldn't stand to hear a moth bawl.

How many ants make a landlord? Ten ants.

Centipedes are found by the hundreds, millipedes by the millions.

Insects have three sets of wings — anterior, posterior and bacteria.

The best place to hold a butterfly is by its borax.

He threw the churn out the window and said, "Oh, look at the butter fly!"

A moth and his wife dined royally on an all-wool spat. Later the moth declined a dinner invitation, saying, "I just had a spat with my wife."

An ant ran pell-mell across the top of a cracker box. Another ant asked, "What's the hurry?" The first ant said, "Can't you read? It says here, 'Tear along dotted line'."

What's worse than a giraffe with a sore throat? A centipede with flat feet.

Cross a moth with a glow-worm and the larvae will find their way around in a dark closet.

Cross a moth with asbestos to get an insect that can fly around a light without getting burned.

A flea is always going to the dogs.

A firefly is all lit up with no place to go.

Two boys pasted together parts of a butterfly, centipede, beetle and grasshopper. They took it to the teacher and said, "What is this?" The teacher asked, "Did you notice whether it hummed when you caught it?" The boys said it did. "Of course," said the teacher, "It's a humbug."

An earthworm is a caterpillar with its fur coat off.

Cross an ant with a parrot and get a walkie-talkie.

Cross a flea with a rabbit for Bugs Bunny.

A stinging letter is when a bee flies out of the envelope.

16
MATHEMATICS

One mathematics book to another: Don't bother me. I have my own problems.

Gross ignorance is worse than ordinary ignorance—144 times worse.

Why do so many churches have plus signs on them?

Student: I know my answer on the test was wrong, but I was close to the correct answer.
Teacher: I know. Only two seats away.

A polygon is a dead parrot.

Geometry teaches one how to move in the best circles.

Father: What are you studying in school?
Son: Guzinta.
Father: Guzinta? What's that?
Son: Like how many times two guzinta four, four guzinta eight.

Zero is a cipher. It has no value itself but adds value to other numerals.

A statistician can lead you by the numbers from a pre-conceived idea to a foregone conclusion.

In school we learn the rule of three, in courtship the rule of two, in marriage the rule of one.

One part of a love triangle is generally a curved leg.

Why is number six afraid of number seven? Seven, eight, nine.

What has three feet, one of them in the middle? A yardstick.

Two's company and three's a crowd. What's four and five? Nine.

Why are mosquitoes good calculators? They add to misery, subtract from pleasure, divide attention and multiply rapidly.

A statistician believes figures don't lie but admits they don't always stand up.

In arithmetic fractions speak louder than words.

When does a mathematician die? When his number is up.

Prove that seven is half of twelve.
Draw a line across the middle of XII and you have VII.

Teacher: Take seven apples from twelve apples. What's the difference?

Student: That's what I say. What's the difference?

___

Teacher: Use the word "geometry" in a sentence.
Student: The little acorn grew and grew. One day it said, "Gee, ahm a tree."

___

Arithmetic is hard work because of all the numbers you have to carry.

___

Do mathematicians' plants have square roots?

___

Father: Did you say your girlfriends' legs are without equal?
Son: No, I said they are without parallel.

___

A zealous young student from Trinity
Derived the tenth root of infinity.
The surfeit of digits
Gave him the fidgets,
So he dropped it and took up divinity.

___

When you add to the truth you subtract from it.

___

A triangle is what happens in a social circle when two are not on the square.

___

2 + 2 = ?
The engineer: 4.
The economist: Not sure. Between 3 and 5.
The lawyer: How much do you want it to be?

___

Seven is an odd number. How do you make it even?
Erase the "s."

An Indian squaw put her six-pound baby on a buffalo hide. The second put hers on an elk hide. The third put her six-pound twins on a hippopotamus hide. The squaw on the hippopotamus equaled the sons of the squaws on the other two hides.

Cardinal numbers are used to count crested red birds.

A slab of stone was discovered with a multiplication problem carved on it. It was the first concrete example.

The first adding machines were so successful they began to multiply.

Aftermath is the period following algebra.

Conic sections are the funny papers.

A sphere is a long, pointed weapon.

A triangle with an angle of 135 degrees is called an obscene triangle.

A circle is a round line with no kinks, joined not to show where it begins.

Algebra was the wife of Euclid.

An axiom is something so obvious it is not necessary to see it.

A circle is a line that meets its other end without ending.

Parallel lines never meet unless you bend them.

You can make a right angle out of a straight line by bisecting the hypothesis.

A circle is a line of no depth running around a dot forever.

_____

Boy to mother: The teacher says something different every day. Yesterday she said five and three make eight; today it's four and four that make eight.

_____

Why don't people ever mention 288? It's two gross.

_____

A man gives one son fifteen cents and the other ten cents. What time is it?
A quarter to two.

_____

What has three feet and can't walk? A yard.

_____

A polygon is a man with many wives.

_____

A converse is approaching a theorem from the rear.

_____

A polygon with seven sides is a hooligan.

_____

Trigonometery is when a lady marries three men at the same time.

_____

A parallelobiped is an animal with parallel feet.

_____

Why did the boy take a ruler to bed? To see how long he slept.

_____

When do 2 and 2 make more than 4? When they make 22.

_____

Where do mathematicians sit at a banquet? At the multiplication table.

A triangle is one figure in mathematics, three in life.

———————————

Some people use statistics the way a drunk uses a lamp post—for support rather than for illumination.

———————————

A converse in geometry is approaching a theorem from the rear.

17
METEOROLOGY

Meteorologists are always shooting the breeze.

Autumn is the season when it's easier to read books because nature turns the leaves.

A bigamist is a dense fog.
AND
Climate is what you do to reach the top of a hill.
AND
A cold front is when you stand with your back to the fireplace.
AND
A cyclone is air in a big rush.

A nightingale is a very windy evening.

Winter is so unpleasant even the wind howls.

A rainbow is always bent on disappearing.

The woman was so charming that even in the rainy season she was mistaken for a cloudless day.

Man phoning the Weather Bureau: I just shoveled eleven inches of "partly cloudy" off my driveway.

The Weather Bureau predicted rain—but mist.

Teacher: The sun is much bigger than the earth.
Student: Then why doesn't it keep the rain off?

A tornado is an act of God? It ought to be called an act of the devil.

He dropped out of the Cycling Club. He preferred to cyclone.

There is a Gael in Shakespeare's "Tempest."

Sign in a store:

AIR CONDITIONED FOR HUMID BEINGS

Herald: Hail to the king!
Subjects: Hail to the king!
King: How dare you hail when I am reigning!

Rain rises again in dew time.

Mother: Thunder and lightning are part of God's work.
Son: It's bedtime. When does God quit work?

Wind is air in a hurry.
AND
Mist is drizzle in slow motion.
AND
Hail is hard-boiled rain.

Smog is a form of air pollution allowing you to see what you're breathing.

A snowflake is a raindrop in ermine.

A storm is a form of weather fit only for conversation.

———

Is the Weather Bureau a non-prophet agency?

———

He's called the weatherman because you don't know weather he's right or wrong.

———

It's really overcast when there's not a sky in the cloud.

———

Mean temperature—Anything below 32 degrees Fahrenheit.

———

A gale is a wind invisible that can make you miserable.

———

A fog is the only thing that's mist even when it's present.

———

Coincide is what you should do when it's raining.

———

Stockbroker: I have a tip for you. It's at fifty now and it will be nearly double that by summer. It's a sure thing.
Customer: I'll buy. What is it?
Stockbroker: The temperature.

———

Amidst—A thick fog.

———

Mean precipitation—Rain falling on Easter bonnets.

———

Weatherman's blooper: Centered in the Midwest is a trough of low pleasure.

———

What's the difference between a cloud and a man who just hit his thumb with a hammer? The cloud pours with rain and the man roars with pain.

Humpty Dumpty had a great fall. It made up for a terrible summer.

When is there a damper on the conversation? When silence reigns.
What color is the wind? Blew.
How do you describe winter weather with two letters.
I. C.

Teacher: What does it mean when the barometer falls?
Student: Whoever nailed it up didn't do a good job.

The man who deals in sunshine
Is the man who gets the crowds;
He gets a lot more business
Than the man who peddles clouds.

Now that hurricanes have both women's and men's names we probably should call them hurricanes and himmicanes.

Climate is weather with a press agent.
AND
A cloudburst has drownpower.
BUT
Drizzle is a cloud with a slow leak.

Judge: Fine today and cooler tomorrow.
Lawyer: Is that a sentence or a weather forecast?

Teacher: How do you spell "weather?"
Student: W-E-T-H-A-R.
Teacher: That's the year's worst spell of weather.

"Did you have a heavy rain here yesterday?"
"Dunno. Didn't weigh it."

Four women tried to walk under one umbrella and none got wet. Why?
It wasn't raining.

It looks like sugar but sweet it's not,
It flies in the air, no wings has got. What is it? Snow.

A man lived west of a chicken yard, east of a glue factory, south of a rubber mill and north of a hog farm. He could tell which way the wind was blowing.

How hot was it? It was so hot we had to feed ice cream to the chickens so the eggs wouldn't come out hard-boiled.

Perhaps tornadoes should be given feminine names. They're spinsters.

Humidity is moisture gone crazy with the heat.

Fog is easy to spell, hard to dispel.

It's raining cats and dogs but it could be worse; it could be hailing taxis.

Why do people ask, "Is it raining outside?" When does it rain inside?

Knock, knock.
Who's there?
Augusta.

August who?
Augusta wind.

A blizzard is a good piece of chicken.

Forecast for the times: Less fair today, even less fair tomorrow.

No wonder life is stormy. It begins with a squall.

Isobars are the same old saloons.

It'a raining cats and dogs. I just stepped in a poodle.

The groom should get a shower. After all, the bride has years of reigning.

A meteorologist is a guy who can look into a girl's eyes and tell whether.

Weather Bureau employee (on phone): I'm sorry, sir, you'll have to call some other bureau. We wouldn't know a war cloud if we saw one.

She couldn't wait for cold weather; she wanted a chap on her hands.

It's raining cats and dogs. No wonder the English call it beastly weather.

The climate is hottest next to the Creator.

Third-grader (on a test): Dew is formed on the grass

when the sun shines down and makes it perspire.

___

Snowflakes are the last of the rugged individualists; no two are alike.

___

Why is the sky blue? Because it isn't green.

___

'S just slush. Snow matter.

___

Why are rainbows like the police? They both appear when the storm is over.

___

When the weatherman predicts terrible weather it's easy to forgive him when he's wrong.

___

The sky should be clearest in big cities because of all the skyscrapers.

___

"I hope the rain keeps up."
"Why? It'll ruin the picnic."
"Not if it keeps up. Only if it comes down."

___

"Hello. Weather Bureau?"
"Yes, this is the Weather Bureau."
"What are the chances of a shower tonight?"
"OK by me, ma'am. Take one if you need it."

___

Noboby can tie a rainbow.

___

Why do we say it's raining cats and dogs? It could be raining reindeer.

___

Sign in a nursery:

CAUTION. THE AIR MAY BE HAZARDOUS
TO YOUR HEALTH.

*"You'll have to call some other Government agency madam . . .
The truth is, we wouldn't know a war-cloud if we saw one . . . "*

The party of daring climbers reached the cold, barren mountain peak to hear the words of the emaciated old man in the cave. He said, "I'm no guru. I just come up here for some fresh air."

The mailman said there was postage dew.

A man in New Zealand found that a blood vessel on his wife's forehead enlarged with the decline of atmospheric pressure. He began predicting with her weather vein.

18
NUTRITION

If you want to get fat, eat fast. If you want to get thin, don't eat; fast.

You'll get indigestion if you swallow your pride and eat crow.

Advertisement:

EAT OUR JAM
KEEP UP ON CURRANT EVENTS

I'm on a sea-food diet. I see food and grab it.

A mint julep is a depth bomb with a southern drawl.

No man can hold liquor as well as a bottle.

Patient: I get a sharp pain in the eye every time I drink coffee.
Doctor: Take the spoon out of the cup.

The chef with a television show was mindful of his peas and cues.

Ohioans and Peruvians, the people of Lima are fine human beans.

"Airline food" is a contradiction in terms.

The bride put her engagement ring in the stew because the recipe called for carrots.

If you were a prisoner with only a calendar and a bed you could eat the dates from the calendar and drink from the springs on the bed.

When the diner ordered lamb chops au gratin the waiter yelled, "Cheese it, the chops.!"

Customer: The chicken you sold me had no wishbone.
Butcher: Madam, our chickens are so happy they have nothing to wish for.

It's a good restaurant, but the prices are so high that when you find a pearl in your oyster you break even.

"It won't be quite like grandma's Thanksgiving dinner, but then-grandma didn't have a microwave!"

Bartender: Our specialty is the "Little David."
Customer: What's it like?
Bartender: We call it "Little David" because it makes you Goliath down.

The breakfast menu listed both pancakes and hotcakes. The customer asked, "Aren't they synonyms?" The waitress said, "No, but if you want synonym I can get you some synonym toast."

What fish goes with peanut butter? Jellyfish.

Age matters a lot—if you're wine or cheese.

His friend recommended the restaurant for its roast beef—but it turned out to be a bum steer.

The salad was excellent. The lettuce was a head of its class.

Smoked herring—kipper of the flame.

From an article on nutritional research: This field of research is so virginal no human eye has ever set foot in it.

Food at a church supper is sacred chow.

Newspaper report of a wine competition: Winners in the homemade claret division were Mrs. Smith (fruity, well-rounded), Mrs. Jones (fine color, full-bodied) and Miss Thomas (slightly acid, will improve if laid down).

A San Antonio restaurant has "Remember the a la mode" pie.

Customer: There's a hair in my turtle soup.
Waiter: Ah, the hare and the turtle, together at last.

Restaurant sign:

WE OFFER PIZZA 'N' QUIET

You'll never starve in the desert because of the sand which is all around you.

She was caught in a traffic jam and a truck gave her a jar.

Customer: How are your tongue sandwiches?
Waiter: They speak for themselves.
Cusomer: Do you serve shrimps here?
Waiter: Yes, we stoop to anything.

You need a certain kind of bee for good health—vitamin B.

A favorite dessert of carpenters and boxers is pound cake.

Most people who buy margarine have seen butter days.

Appetizers are what you keep eating until you ruin your appetite.

Whoever thought of the word "doughnuts" was a poor judge of nuts.

Customer: Waiter, this spicy food is giving me heartburn.
Waiter: What did you expect—sunburn?

New cook: My sponge cake didn't turn out right.
Old cook: What's wrong with it?
New cook: They sent me those new plastic sponges.

Diner: This chicken must have been an incubator chicken.
Waiter: I don't know what you mean.
Diner: No chicken that had a mother's care could be this tough.

Diner: Is this tea or coffee? It tastes like turpentine.
Waiter: I assure you it's coffee. Our tea tastes like dish water.

Diner: Do you think raw oysters are healthy?
Waiter: I'm sure of it. I've never heard one complain.

Waiter: That's bean soup.
Diner: I don't care what it's been, what is it now?

Diner: I want coffee without cream.
Waiter: We're out of cream. Will you take it without milk?

It's no good knowing of a restaurant where you can eat dirt cheap. Who wants to eat dirt?

Unlike a child, an egg gets beaten only when it's good.

Molasses and trousers are both thinner in hot weather and thicker in cold.

A waffle is a pancake with a non-skid tread.

Leftovers—they're here today and here tomorrow.

Waiter: I recommend the hash. The cook puts all he's got into it.

Gelatin dessert quivers because the cook makes it with hot water, then puts it on ice.

Fish is brain food because fish spend their lives in schools.

Chef—A man for all seasonings.

Salt is useful in a pinch.

Man does not live by bread alone. Hence, the sandwich.

Whatever is worth doing should be well done—with the exception of steak.

Dieter's maxim: Don't count the minutes at the table—just the seconds.

Coffee is a break fluid.

Advertisement for beer: "Rhapsody in brew."

Advertisement for whiskey:"You'll like it. We've got the proof."

Advertisement for a soft drink: "You be the judge. Try a case."

Advertisement for orange juice: "Swallow our pride."

19
OCEANOGRAPHY

Oceanography is a study in depth.

An oceanographer is a scientist to whom the ocean's bottom is more important than the moon's behind.

Piracy on the high seas is a crime wave.

"How are your grades?"
"They're underwater."
"What does that mean?"
"They're below C level."

The law is like an ocean; all the trouble is caused by breakers.

The summer resort closed because the tide went out and never came back.

The lowest ebb is not the turn of the tide.

Why is the ocean restless? You would be too, if you had rocks and lobsters in your bed.

What do two oceans say when they meet? Long time, sea.

Why was the ocean arrested? It beat up on the shore.

Man has a new interest in oceanography—now that he can barely keep his head above water.

Ocean romance—Where buoys meet gulls.

Newly-weds were walking along the beach. The husband said, "Roll on, thou deep and dark blue ocean, roll!" His wife said, "It's doing it, you wonderful man."

The ocean is so polluted that one day the tide will go out and won't come back in. It'll call in sick.

Does the ocean have dates? Yes, it goes out with the tide.

What would you use to cut an ocean in two? A see-saw.

What doesn't get wet, no matter how much it rains? The ocean.

Why does the ocean get angry at ships? Because they cross it so much.

20
PHYSICS

There was a young lady from Bright
Whose speed was much faster than light.
She set out one day
In a relative way,
And returned the previous night.

"Don't go faster than sound. I want to talk!"

Judge: Your name and occupation?
Defendant: My name is Sparks. I'm an electrician.
Judge: What's the charge?
Defendant: I'm charged with battery.
Judge: Put this man in a dry cell.

Nothing is heavier than lead.
Rubber balloons are heavier than nothing.
Ergo, rubber balloons are heavier than lead.

Television has changed children. They used to be irresistible forces; now they're immovable bodies.

Lovers keep rediscovering the secret of perpetual emotion.

The fission fragments of uranium atoms are fission chips.

Judge: You are charged with going 45 miles an hour in a 30-miles-per-hour speed zone.
Defendant: That's ridiculous. I wasn't even out for an hour.

If the apple hadn't fallen we'd have Newton's law of levitation.

You'll be thought cool
If you call it the joule,
But there'll be a howl
If you call it the jowl.

The atom was split in the 40's and we still don't know if it was a wisecrack.

"It was our agent's idea. We have to use a colorimeter to make sure our blues are up to par."

Reprinted with permission of Markson Science.

A man read an announcement about a two-day course for airplane pilots. He called the Aircraft Owners and Pilots Association and said, "I'd like more information about your crash course." The reply was, "We don't even use that word."

———

Ohm. That's what there's no place like.

———

Teacher: Water always runs downhill.
Student: I didn't even know it could walk.

———

Teacher: How would you describe a void—an absolute nothing?
Student: A balloon with its skin off.

———

Heat travels faster than cold. A person can catch a cold.

In nuclear warfare all men are cremated equal.

If we go metric will we have to give up the pinch, the dab, the smidgin and the dollop?

A shadow is the only thing that never casts a shadow.

Even a man of steel is no good if he loses his temper.

Time is nature's way of keeping everything from happening at once.

What can you say about a vacuum? There's nothing to it.

Two men were contemplating a sculpture of a woman. Its title was "Echo." The first said, "Echo in the legend was a woman because a woman always has the last word." The second said, "There's something wrong with the legend. An echo speaks only when spoken to."

There was a girl from New York
Whose body was lighter than cork.
She had to be fed
For six weeks on lead
Before she went out for a walk.

The scientist who swallowed uranium got atomic ache.

Man has progressed from huntin' to fission.

Ben Franklin discovered electricity after his wife told him to go fly a kite.

A scientist visited Los Angeles for a week. When asked

to describe its atmosphere he said, "Can a fish describe the murky water in which it swims?"

He fell into the lens grinding machine and made a spectacle of himself.

For every action there is an equal and opposite criticism.

A skydiver is a dropout.

Gram—Intense review for an exam.
Torque—Conversation
Program—Movement for adoption of the metric system.

It's easy for a physicist to have too many ions in the fire.

" . . . and why do you feel the lab is stinting on containers for cryogenic work?"

An atom is a very small thing that becomes one of the biggest when split.

Human history is the story from split Adam to split atom.

A live wire makes hay with the grass that others let grow under their feet.

A strapless gown manifests the struggle between gravity and personal magnetism.

Why does lightning shock people? It doesn't know how to conduct itself.

When are eyes not eyes? When cold air makes them water.

What makes a candle uncomfortable? Glowing pains.

What pain do we make light of? Windowpane.

Sound is a rapid series of osculations. That's how a man and woman make beautiful music together.

Summer days are longer because heat expands them.

The three states of water are high water, low water and breakwater.

Erg—What you do to motivate people; you erg them on.

Woman to auto mechanic:
I have a short circuit. Can you lengthen it while I wait?

Electricians are always up on current events.

A man came home and saw his wife walking on the ceiling. "Don't you know that's against the law of gravity?" he yelled. She fell to floor and said,"You had to open your big mouth."

"Why doesn't someone tell him the atomic bomb has already been invented?"

There's a notable family named Stein.
There's Gertrude, there's Ep and there's Ein.
Gert's prose is the bunk,
Ep's sculpture is junk
And no one can understand Ein.

Molecule—A vision-correcting lens worn on one eye.

A boy raking leaves and sticks from the yard was heard

to say, "Issac Newton, I hate you."

The main difference between air and water is that you can make air wetter but you can't make water wetter.

With an X-ray machine you can see things in people where others can't.

The metric system refers to kilograms, centigrams and telegrams.

When a body is immersed in water the telephone rings.

What's matter? Never mind. What's mind? No matter.

Turning water into steam or steam into water is called conversation.

A liter is a nest of kittens.

A magnet is a worm that turns into a fly.

Atom is Eve's husband.

Inertia is the ability to rest.

Gravity is what you get when you eat too fast.

Vacuum is an empty place where the Pope lives.

An optimistic gardener believes what goes down must come up.

A thermometer is an instrument for raising temperature.

Lightning never strikes twice in the same place because when lightning strikes, that place isn't there anymore.

Tension—What the sergeant shouts to the troops.

Teacher: Can you explain how the telephone works?
Student: It's like a long dog; step on its tail in Chicago and it barks in New York.
Teacher: How does the radio work?
Student: It works the same way, only without the dog.

Man watching boxing match: Hit him now! "You've got the wind with you."

Ideals are like tuning forks. You must sound them frequently to keep your mind up to pitch and your life in tune.

The difference between lightning and electricity is that lightning is free.

A man who ate candy constantly and never brushed his teeth wound up with so many cavities he talked with an echo.

Why does it take longer to go from second base to third than from first base to second? Between second and third there's a shortstop.

"Magnets" is an example of a collective noun.

For every action there's a reaction; for every pun there's a groan.

"The dawn of a new era, gentlemen, withe the first meal cooked by Atomic energy . . . 'Fission Chips', naturally! . . . "

From a student essay: When a warm object is placed

in contact with a cool object they both come to the same temperature by heart transfer.

From a scientific paper: Ultraviolent spectroscopy shows its composition.

A newspaper ad listed fans for ten cents; it was an obvious typographical error. When a woman came into the store and demanded a ten-cent fan the manager handed her a piece of cardboard and told her to hold it steady while turning her head as fast as possible.

What do electricians have for breakfast? Probably ohmlettes.

People are shorter in the morning because they've been magnetized through the night.

Molecular motion as a source of mechanical energy is inefficient because of the resistance of the molecule Moe Shun.

Cathodes are kittens that can sing.

The atom bomb project at Oak Ridge, Tennessee during WW II was top secret. Among the dozens of rumors in the new city was that the plant was making the front halves of horses, to be shipped to Washington, D. C. for assembly.

Momentum—What you give a person the day he leaves to work somewhere else.

The electrician is currently in a cell in a state of shock,

waiting for the arrival of the circuit judge. Although the electrician conducts himself well, he refuses food and protests, "Wire my insulate? Watt have I done? It wasn't my volt. I want to go ohm."

From a textbook: For many quantum systems, for example atoms with less energy than that needed to detach the least strongly bound electron into the energy continuum, most measurements of dynamical quantities yield only one set of discrete values, the eigenvalues of the appropriate Schrodinger equation or its equivalent in the Heisenberg matrix formalism. Everybody knows that.

A farmer, when asked the difference between radiation and contamination, said, "Radiation is when you smell manure; contamination is when you step in it."

Acoustic—The instrument used in shooting pool.

The first place to shop for electrical equipment is an outlet store.

When a policeman stops you for speeding, remember he's heard them all. Don't say you were pushed by a strong tailwind.

What can you say about a guy who drives his new truck off a cliff to test his air brakes?

The atom bomb is here to stay — but are we?

Student: "Toboggan is not something you do on an inclined plane."
Teacher: "What is it?"

Student: "It's what you do to get the price down."

———————

Advertisement of a gas company: "Gas it BTU-tiful."

21
PSEUDOSCIENCE

A haunted wigwam is a creepy teepee.

Insurance salesman: Who is to be your beneficiary?
Customer: Myself. I believe in reincarnation.

If you carry a rabbit's foot for good luck, don't forget what it did for the rabbit.

Fortune teller to apprentice:
Tell every unmarried woman there's a man in her future and tell every married woman there's a future in her man.

"Sometimes I wish they'd be a little more discriminating about who they hand these research grants to."

Reprinted with permission of Markson Science.

163

A medium is a big wheel with spooks.

A seance is a good experience if you hit a happy medium.

Seances are publicized by a spooksman.

A psychic ought to charge medium prices.

A fortune teller who saw an ambulance in her crystal ball told the customer, "Your little boy will be a doctor — or maybe a lawyer."

High spirits are ghosts that haunt skyscrapers.

A haunting melody is a popular tune played on a ghost-to-ghost network.

A spiritual lift is a haunted elevator.

A psychopath is a crazy road.

A bat boy is a vampire's son.

One angel to another: Do you believe in the heretofore?

When the witch doctor began his song and dance the patient said, "What the hex are you up to?"

Telepathy is a communications medium invented by Samuel F. B. Morse.

Where does a ghost pick up its mail? At the dead letter office.

Why did the witch flunk out of school? She just couldn't spell.

What kind of cheese did Mary Queen of Scots eat? Loch Ness Munster.

A photographer tried to document the existence of a ghost by taking its picture. The ghost posed obligingly, but nothing appeared on the negative. The spirit was willing but the flash was weak.

Two seers were caught in a storm. One said to the other, "This reminds me of Hurricane Murgatroyd to come in 2026."

When the gentleman ghost got fresh with the lady ghost she said, "Get your hands off me!" "Lighten up," said the gentleman ghost, "I'm only doing what comes supernaturally."

A housewife reincarnated as a clock kept saying, "Please, I only have two hands."

From a patent application:
For a corpse that comes to life, a bell that can be rung from inside the coffin. Also, a ladder, in case the corpse regains enough energy to climb out under its own power.

Many a hiccup is a message from departed spirits.

Spiritualism is gnome man's land.

A demon is a ghoul's best friend.

A spiritualist is a trance guesser.

The difference between spirit doctors and doctored spirits is that the latter really shows you the next world.

Overheard in a singles bar:
"Under what sign were you conceived"
"Keep off the grass."

I don't know if there's life after death, but I'm bringing along a change of underwear.

One ghost to another; Do you really believe in human beings?

The person who can really bring you in contact with the spirit world is your bartender.

A clairvoyant knows where the candle is when the lights go out.

In palmistry a fortune teller palms herself off as a hand reading expert.

A witch doctor is a sinister minister.

A witch is a hexpert.

A seance is a spirited session.

An astrologer must know the date of your birth — and not only that, but the exact time of day — before telling you what you want to hear.

A witch is a flying sorcerer.

_____

A comma is what a medium goes into.

_____

A ghost keeps its car in a mirage.

_____

Spiritualism is seance fiction.

_____

Paranormal is a couple of regular guys.

_____

Doctor: Under my treatment you will be a new man.
Patient: Send the bill to the new man.

_____

Patient: Hurry, Doctor, I'm at death's door.
Doctor: Don't worry, I'll pull you through.

_____

"Do you believe the souls of animals can enter human beings?"
"Yes. I lent you a thousand dollars and never got it back. I was an ass."

_____

A man who consulted a medium expected serious responses to his questions. When the medium laughed at everything he said, the man hit her. "Sorry," he said, "but my mother taught me always to hit a happy medium."

_____

"I went to see a spiritualist."
"Any good?"
"No. Just medium."

_____

A woman established contact with her late husband through a spiritualist. "Are you happy?" she asked. "Oh, yes," came the answer. "The pastures are green. It's indeed a beautiful world. The females are gorgeous. They have sleek, rounded forms and their eyes speak of love." The woman said, "I hope some day I can join you in heaven." "Heaven?" said the man. "Who said I was in heaven? I'm a bull in Montana."

A happy medium is a good-natured spiritualist.

The afterlife is the one place you go without having to pack.

"Psychic?"
"Yes, seer."

The spiritualist guaranteed to bring her husband back at a seance. But the wife claimed it was all a fake because her husband had never, never, never smelled of garlic!

22
TECHNOLOGY

The very first chair was made for a king. It was throne out.

What driver needs no license? A screwdriver.

My family is in iron and steel. My Ma irons and my Pa steals.

"Look at the holes in this board."
"They're knot holes."
"If they're not holes, what are they?"

What coat has no buttons and is always put on wet? A coat of paint.

A man who died from drinking varnish had a beautiful finish.

Where does steel wool come from? From sheep that live in Iron Mountain.

The electric bill is the charge of the light brigade.

The electrician is always wiring for money.

Gutenberg created the typographical era.

Edison proved the road to success is paved with good inventions.

Hargreaves invented a machine for spinning cotton threads. He called it a jenny in honor of his wife. Crompton invented a similar machine. He called it a mule.

Ancient Egyptian writing is called hydraulics.

An alarm clock is OK if you like that sort of ting.

Color is fast only when it doesn't run.

Teacher: Where is your homework?
Student: I made a paper airplane out of it and someone hijacked it.

A digital watch doesn't run clockwise.

The man who invented rope built a huge hempire.

The inventor of the cigarette lighter became flamous.

The first telephone conversation was between people only eighteen feet apart. It was a close call.

"Behold! The first girdle."
"Does it work?"
"Of corset does."

Knock, knock.
Who's there?
Carson.

Carson who?
Carson the road have polluted the air.

What goes up and down at the same time? Stairs.

Where do dressmakers build their houses? In the outskirts.

Two wrongs don't make a right but two Wrights make an airplane.

What we need is a device built so that frustrated people can cuss into a mike and what comes out is happy talk.

Today's executives have an infinite capacity for taking planes.

A plumber's helper is a wrench hand.

What goes, "tick-tick choo, tick-tick choo?" A clock with a cold.

What kind of nail cannot be hammered? A fingernail.

What kind of shoe is made from a banana peel? A slipper.

What is the difference between AC and DC? AC is for around the city and DC is for distant countries.

Adhesive tape is a sticky cassette.

A muffler is what keeps a car warm in winter.

"We can't claim another giant stride forward for science on THIS one, professor . . . it was just a gas leak in the basement . . . "

A knob is a thing to a door.

———————

A coal miner is a vein man.

———————

To go to a foreign country you need a visa. For a round trip you need a visa versa.

———————

What is the world's greatest invention? Man: the wheel. Teenager: the telephone. Housewife: the self-cleaning oven.

———————

Of all the machines in the world, only the bicycle comes male and female.

———————

Mix sawdust with pectin to make a logjam.

———————

An eskimo's house without a bathroom is an ig. No loo.

———————

A door is not a door when it's ajar.

———————

Petroleum exploration can be a crude awakening.

———————

Does a watch tell time if it doesn't talk?

———————

Sign in an electric generating plant:

WE HAVE THE POWER
TO MAKE YOU SEE THE LIGHT

———————

Swift, in Gulliver's Travels, mentions an architect who tries to build houses from the roof downward. That's as bad as the textile designer who tried to get spiders to spin colored webs.

When the clock strikes thirteen what time is it? Time to get the clock fixed.

What the driver needs today is a transmission that automatically shifts the blame.

The first lubricant for wheels was caster oil.

The detective tried to match the fingerprints but they were whorls apart.

You can walk on water if you add some sand and cement.

What did the digital watch say to its mother? "Look, Ma, no hands!"

What kind of tunes do you get from a car? Cartoons.

The automobile had good shock observers.

Plumbers are drain surgeons.

Bakers are wealthy; they roll in dough.

He wrote a book about watch making and everybody said it was about time.

Somebody ought to invent: A spray to stop floors squeaking; a noiseless soup spoon; an alarm clock that doesn't ring but emits the odor of bacon and coffee; a spot remover that removes spots left by other spot removers.

Diesel fitter—What a pantyhose salesman says.

Some minds are like concrete — thoroughly mixed and permanently set.

"Is the Xerox machine running down the hall?"
"Nope. It just sits there."

"How does television work?"
"I don't know. There are no wires."
"So—with wires you would understand?"

Engineer's testimony in traffic court: Due to circumstances beyond my control the wheels accelerated in one plane while the force of gravity operated at an angle to the rotating plane. This produced a rotation perpendicular to the plane of the wheel rotation. In other words, my car skidded.

When is a car not a car? When it turns into a garage.

How can you determine the height of a building with the help of a barometer? Lower the barometer from the roof on a string, then measure the length of the string.

At a trade fair in an underdeveloped country a company demonstrated an automated meat processor. A pig was put in and out came sausages. The natives were not impressed. They wanted a machine where sausages were put in and out came pigs.

The husband asked the wife how she was able to mow the lawn by herself using the new lawnmower. She said that the handle indicated that three hard pulls would start the machine. He observed the notation 3 H.P. on the handle.

An air conditioner regulated the temperature and moisture in the air for humid beings.

The hairdresser was told that if his customers ate bullets they would come out as bangs.

The first chair was made especially for royalty but it was throne out.

A new type of clock can run through summer, fall and winter, without winding, because it has no spring.

He had a glut feeling that there would be plenty of petroleum..

The automobile had good shock observers.

The fringe benefits of technology:
The railroad, automobile and airplane teach the value of time; lose one minute and you may be too late. The telegraph demonstrates the significance of speech; every word has a price. The telephone, radio and television bring people together; what we say is carried to all parts of the earth.

The iron age occurred before drip-dry clothes were introduced.

23
UFOs

"We want six containers of atomic absorption standard solution. Two black, one with cream, one with cream and sugar . . . "

A flying saucer is one dish that is truly out of this world.

———————

Two men were sailing along on a flying carpet and one said to the other, "No, I don't believe in flying saucers."

UFO? No comet.

A UFO landed in a nudist colony. The pilot emerged, walked up to a lady and said, "Take me to your tailor."

A UFO landed in the Black Hills of South Dakota. The crew and pasengers stared at the sculptured faces of four presidents for a few minutes and the captain said, "Nonsense. This is just your imagination."

After a lengthy survey of the earth, one passenger of a UFO said to another, "Let's come back when the meek inherit the earth."

UFO pilot to space shuttle pilot: How many miles do you get to the gallon?

UFO pilot reading the New York Times: "Hey, here's a report saying we don't exist!"

UFO passenger arguing with another: "Oh, go to Earth!"

Report of an extraterrestrial after a visit to the earth:
Of the ten earthlings I approached, four thought I was running for political office, three thought I was selling a new product, two thought I was promoting a new television program and one gave me a dollar.

UFO pilot to crew, looking at the earth: You'd think there were villages, roads and farms down there. Actually, it's nothing more than marsh gas.

UFO pilot to co-pilot, staring at a jet airplane: Now do you believe in flying cigars?

"Take me to your Ambassador."

A three-headed creature from a UFO walked up to a human and said, "Don't just stand there. Run and get your camera."

An eight-armed creature from a UFO took over a fruit stand. One customer said, "He may look weird, but he's getting two dollars a pound for grapes."

Lady (to a three-legged, nine-armed creature at her door): No, I don't believe in UFOs.

An extraterrestrial saw a man hit the jackpot on a slot machine. Hundreds of quarters poured out. The ET patted the slot machine and said, "You'd better do something for that cold."

The first things the UFO pilot encountered on earth were a mailbox and fire alarm box. He reported, "The dumpy fellow with the big mouth doesn't say a word. The red character just screams his head off."

The National Aeronautics and Space Administration plans to put 500 cattle into orbit. It will be the herd shot round the world.

Men can walk more safely in space than in many city streets.

How do you slake your thirst in space? Drink from the Big Dipper.

How do ETs drink their tea? From flying saucers.

Martian to American Secretary of State: We're here by accident. We didn't planet this way.

An ET with three noses and five eyes walked up to a man and said, "I want to see your leader." The man replied, "Nonsense. You want to see a plastic surgeon."

A pale, shaken woman told her husband, "There was an extraterrestrial robot in the kitchen today." He asked, "Did it hurt you?" "No," she said, "but it eloped with my blender."

A Martian visiting Earth saw a garbage can fall off a truck. The truck didn't stop. The Martian grabbed the can and ran after the truck, shouting, "Hey, lady, you dropped your purse."

The pilot of a UFO encountered a second grade student. The pilot tried to communicate with a geometric formula, "Pi r squared," said the pilot. "No, dummy," the student responded. "Pie are round . . . cornbread is square."

24
ZOOLOGY

One version of evolution: Call it a dress at $29.99, a gown at $159.99 and a creation at $1599.

Teacher: In order for the species to survive, animals must breed.
Student: Of course, if they didn't breed they'd suffocate.

I'm a horse but I can't eat hay and I can't run. What am I? A sea horse.

What's as big as an elephant and doesn't weigh an ounce?
An elephant's shadow.

What season do kangaroos like best? Springtime.

Teacher: Would you say a snail is strong?
Student: Yes, it carries its house on its back.

Teacher: Why does the giraffe have such a long neck?
Student: Because its head is so far from its body.

A tourist admired an Indian chief's necklace. She asked, "What is it made of?" "Alligator teeth," he said. She shuddered. Regaining her composure, she said, "I suppose they hold the same meaning for you that pearls do or us." He said, "Not quite. Anybody can open an oyster."

Amphibians are animals that tell lies.

A lion tamer's whip is an animal cracker.

A fish with a deep voice is a bass.

A grouchy violinist is a fiddler crab.

Groundhog is sausage.

Deer are wealthy; they're known for their bucks.

Ground beef is a cow sitting on the grass.

A horse can't say yes — only neigh.

A pride of lions, a herd of buffalo, a flock of geese. What is the word for a group of mink? A fur coat.

Nobody likes a skunk because it puts on such awful airs.

The female kangaroo knows what's in her bag without looking.

What is a sleeping bull? A bulldozer.

Why was the pig named Ink? It kept running out of the pen.

Why do baby pigs eat so much? They have to make hogs of themselves.

How do you make a tortoise fast? Take its food away.

What's the difference between a counterfeit bill and an angry rabbit? The bill is bad money and the rabbit is a mad bunny.

Why does a dog wag its tail? Nobody will wag it for him.

What is taller sitting down than standing up? A dog.

A person taking a bath is like what animal? A little bear.

What's the worst weather for mice? When it's raining cats and dogs.

"Call your dog off!"
"I can't. I call him Butch and it's too late to change his name now."

What's the difference between a cat and a comma? A cat has its claws at the end of its paws and the comma has its pause at the end of its clause.

When a fish leaves school it's ready for the reel world.

He didn't buy Christmas seals because he didn't know what to feed them.

One day I went out to the zoo,
For I wanted to see the old gnu.
But the old gnu was dead,
And the new gnu, they said,
Surely knew as a gnu he was new.

In what way is the pig most unusual? First you kill him, then you cure him.

A fox is a chick who gets a mink from a wolf.

Dogma is a bitch with puppies.

A taxidermist is a guy who knows his stuff.

How do you keep your puppy from smelling? Hold its nose.

There was a sightseer named Sue
Who saw a strange beast at the zoo.
When she asked, "Is it old?"
She was smilingly told,
"It's not an old beast, but a gnu."

What does a cow say when it's sad? Moo hoo hoo.

Cross the Loch Ness monster with a shark and get Loch Jaw.

The medium was late to a seance because of poor tranceportation.

Barnacles are ship huggers.

A zebra is a horse behind bars.

A tired kangaroo is out of bounds.

A crab is a fiddler on the reef.

An oyster is a fish built like a nut.

In heaven the sheep and goats will be divided, but on earth the sheep are usually the goats.

"Do you get fur from skunks?"
"I get just as fur as I can."

Leap year is the best time for a kangaroo.

A horse eats best when it doesn't have a bit in its mouth.

A mole can make molehills out of mountains.

A primate is the spouse of a prime minister.

A rabbit is very timid, but no cook can make it quail.

A stag is sometimes forced to run for deer life.

A bullfrog is no miracle; a thistle is no miracle; even a bird singing is no miracle. But a bullfrog sitting on a thistle singing like a bird is a miracle.

Aspersion is a donkey from Persia.

An ibex is at the back of a book.

An octopus is a person who expects the best.

The snake that curled up on the automobile windshield became known as the windshield viper.

What animal devours its older relatives? An ant eater.

One must strip off their genes to determine the sex of a chromoson.

A zoologist tried to produce a squalone by crossbreeding a squid with an abalone. But something went wrong with the experiment and the offspring turned out to be an abalid.

Knock, knock.
Who's there?
Who.
Who's who?
You're an owl.

Prayer does not always signify a person is religious. Are lions religious because they are often out preying?

Teacher: "In what country are elephants found?"
Student: "They have good memories. They don't get lost."

Why did the impatient fish hop on another fish?
To travel faster on down the pike.

A sponge is the only thing full of holes that holds water.

A zoo is a place where people may visit but animals are barred.

An animal is a tail bearer.

What is the difference between elephants and fleas?

Elephants can have fleas but fleas cannot have elephants.

The cow caught cold and all it could give was ice cream.

Men's eyes are like birds, flitting from limb to limb.

The elephant travels with more luggage than other animals; it always has its trunk. The fox and rooster travel with the least luggage; between them they have only a comb and brush.

A frog is extremely sensitive. Just touch it and it will croak.

A camel with one hump married a camel with two humps. Their first baby had no humps. They called him Humphrey.

It's aardvark but it's a living.

An antelope is the runaway marriage of an aunt.

What's the difference between an oyster and a baby? The oyster makes his bed in the ocean and the baby makes its ocean in the bed.

How do you get down from an elephant? You don't. You get down from a goose.

What do elephants have that no other animals have? Baby elephants.

Why do elephants have short tails? So they won't get caught in subway doors.

He put hay under his pillow to feed his nightmares.

The automobile did away with the horse but not with the ass.

"Is the milk pasteurized?"
"Yes, the cows are put out to pasture every morning."

Is a goatee a small goat?

A man who worked like a horse complained subtly to his boss, "Can I go to my stall and hit the hay?"

On a modern dairy farm cows have calves without any contact with bulls. This is called artificial inspiration.

"Look at that bunch of cows."
"Not bunch — herd."
"Heard what?"
"I mean a cow herd."
"Who cares? I don't have any secrets from them."

Driving sheep over your frozen pond is pulling wool over your ice.

It's a mistake to gossip in the stable because the horses carry tails.

Fish get chicken pox on a small scale.

The veterinarian gave the pig some oinkment.

A goblet is a female turkey.

A skunk is the scenter of attention.

"Does the hen lay or lie?"
"Lift her up and see."

The zoo keeper went through the cage of lethargic sea lions carrying seagulls, which he fed to the promiscuous dolphins. He was arrested for carrying gulls across staid lions for immoral porpoises.

The veterinarian gave the rabbit some hare tonic.

Hannibal crosses the Alps with elephants and what did he get?
He got mountains that remember everything.

A camel is a horse designed by a committee.

The waters receded and Noah released the animals. Two snakes stayed behind. Noah said, "Go forth and multiply." They refused to go. They were adders.

The rhinoceros never toots his own horn.

An oyster can produce a pearl of great value — if it has a little grit.

The elephant lives to a ripe old age without worrying about his weight.

The whale never gets into trouble until he comes up and spouts off.

A turtle makes no progress until he sticks his neck out.

———————

The woodpecker never gets anywhere by knocking. He pecks away until he finishes the job and he owes his success to the fact that he uses his head.

———————

The stag never asks for another's doe.

———————

Cats have only nine lives; frogs croak every night.

———————

For a gift that keeps on giving, give a pair of rabbits.

———————

"That's a camel's hair brush."
"It must take him a long time to brush his hair."

———————

Policeman: What are you doing here?
Biologist: Looking for flora and fauna.
Policeman: Move along or I'll run you in along with your girl friends.

———————

Teacher: What animals belong to the cat family?
Student: Father cat, mother cat and the kittens.

———————

What animals are keys that don't open locks? Monkey, turkey and donkey.

———————

A caterpillar is an upholstered worm.

———————

How does a pig build a house? He just ties a knot in his tail and he has a pig's tie.

———————

A horse has six legs — the forelegs in front and the two behind.

The pony wasn't really sick; he was just a little hoarse.

_____

A parasite is the murder of an infant.

_____

An emu is the purring made by a cat.

_____

Bald heads are wrongly called bear places.

_____

When does a boy become like a bear? In the summer when he's bearfooted.

_____

A blubber mouth is a gossipy whale.

_____

Once upon a time a fish lodged in the ear of a whale until he caused a herring problem.

_____

A mermaid is a deep she fish.

_____

The butcher makes both ends meat.

_____

One ram said to the other "After ewe."

_____

A good milk cow can be identified by her rudder.

_____

The most unusual fish is the piano tuna.

_____

Apiary is a house for apes.

_____

Why do elephants have trunks? Because they don't have suitcases.

Sadly shellfish is a creature who frequently has a crab for a mate.

_____

Vanity, vanity—even rabbits can have false hare.

Books by Morris Goran

Introduction to the Physical Sciences, Glencoe, IL: Free Press, 1959.

Experimental Chemistry for Boys, New York: John F. Rider Publisher, 1961.

Experimental Biology for Boys, New York: John F. Rider Publisher, 1961.

Experimental Astronautics, Indianapolis, Ind: Howard W. Sams, 1967.

Experimental Earth Sciences, Indianapolis, Ind: Howard W. Sams, 1967.

The Core of Physical Science, Chicago, IL: Cimarron Publishers, 1967.

Experimental Chemistry, London, England: Lutterworth, 1967.

The Story of Fritz Haber, Norman, OK: University of Oklahoma Press, 1967.

Biologia Experimental, Barcelona, Spain: Ramon Sopena, 1967.

The Future of Science, New York: Sparton Books, 1971.

Science and Anti-Science, Ann Arbor, Mich: Ann Arbor Science Publishers, 1974.

A Preface to Astronomy, Westport, Conn: Technomic Publishers, 1975.

The Modern Myth: Ancient Astronauts and UFOs, Cranbury, N.J.: A. S. Barnes, 1978.

Fact, Fraud and Fantasy: The Occult and Pseudosciences, Cranbury, N.J.: A. S. Barnes, 1979.

Ten Lessons of the Energy Crisis, Newton, Mass.: Environmental Design and Research Center, 1980.

Conquest of Pollution, Newton, Mass.: Environmental Design and Research Center, 1981.

Can Science Be Saved? Saratoga, Cal.: Rand E Publishers, 1981.

The Past of Western Science, Chicago, IL: Cimarron Publishers, 1984.

The Lure of Longevity (with Marjorie Goran), Saratoga, Cal: Rand E Publishers, 1984.

A Guide To The Perplexed About Pseudoscience: Chicago, IL: Cimarron Publishers, 1985.

Acknowledgements

Thanks are due to the following individuals and organizations for permission to reprint certain of the cartoons in this collection.

David C. Simonson of Pioneer Press Newspaper, 1232 Central Avenue, Wilmette, Illinois 60091.

The Catalogue of Softwear Unltd., P.O. Box 265, Twisp, Washington 98856, Creators of humorous and intellectual designs available on T-shirts and posters.

Markson Science, 7815 So. 46th St., P.O. Box 8017, Phoenix, AZ.

News American Syndicate, 1703 Kaiser Ave., P.O. Box 19620, Irvine, CA. From Grin and Bear It by George Lichty.

Ambassador East, 1301 North State Parkway, Chicago, Illinois.